The Book on Pro Wrestling

Lessons from Rip Rogers

By Caleb Hall

FOREWORD

Caleb Hall, long time student of Rip Rogers
Founder, Dubai Pro Wrestling

In honor of the man who gave so much to this business we love, and helped so many turn a passion into a career through his guidance.

This book could very well save your life. A bold statement about a pro wrestling book, but yet still very possible. When I was wrestling, I took a lot of unnecessary risks. Mimicking sometimes exactly what I had seen Rey Mysterio Jr. and other high flyers do in their matches. I thought that because I was much smaller than most of the other guys in pro wrestling, that I had to do a lot more of the high risk moves to get noticed.

I was getting good responses from fans after my matches and what I was doing seemed to be working as a wrestler starting out and trying to get recognition. I kept looking to top what I had done previously with more exciting and sometimes more dangerous moves because I thought that was what made for a great match. It wasn't until I met Rip Rogers at OVW that I learned I had it almost entirely wrong. Not too say that I should have never tried to pull off high flying exciting moves, but knowing when, where, and why to use them, if I was going to use them at all, was what I was missing.

Having now been involved in the business in one form or another for nearly 20 years, I've met many people who, like me, thought that dangerous high risk moves were the way to get noticed. And for some, taking those risks have in large part skyrocketed their careers. On the other side of that coin, some of them have been seriously injured performing those moves, and more unfortunately, some of them have even died.

After training for years with Rip Rogers, things that I had never even thought of before, that once revealed to me by him, seemed so common sense.

This is a collection of teachings by Rip Rogers through twitter posts, youtube videos, personal discussions with him, and years of Rip's OVW class, made into one easy to read book. Generations of knowledge passed from Rip's mentors The Poffo's, Lanny and Randy (Randy "Macho Man" Savage) to Rip and then on to the next generation, compiled here for you, the reader, to easily access this invaluable knowledge to better your understanding of this great business so that you may avoid pitfalls and problems, already experienced by others, to help you further your career.

I come into this world with nothing. I will leave this world with nothing. Now, how many lives can I influence to help them get to their dream.

Rip Rogers

The lessons here will be categorized into sections from selling, to tag matches, to promoting, and more, so that readers can easily access whatever bits of information they are looking for.

The man, the legend "Hustler" Rip Rogers! What can I say... An absolute honour to have had the opportunity to learn from one of the best brains in the wrestling business. I first arrived at OVW in October of 2003 after a successful tryout camp earlier in the year in which Jim Cornette invited me to join Nick Dinsmore's class. It was only a couple of months when myself and fellow Brit Steve Lewington (DJ Gabriel) were asked to join the Developmental/Advance class, training with Rip and the contract talent.

This was very daunting to say the least, as a young lad low on confidence being a little fish in a big pond. From day one however, Rip was very welcoming, straight to the point, and knew how to build someone's confidence. Rip would drill you for hours on end. Repetition, repetition, repetition. Putting you in all types of situations and make you think on your feet while also implementing a "think shoot and work" attitude.

I owe Rip so much, not only for pushing me to be the best I could be, but for helping me be over prepared, and to get my skills recognized and praised by those high up in WWE years down the line.

My last trip to OVW was in the summer of 2011 before I moved down to Florida. I'll always remember at OVW TV Rip pulling me to one side. He said "You have been doing this a long time and I want to help you. I want you to send William Regal your stuff and I will recommend you." He passed me Regal's contact information and wrote a note of recommendation to "The

Lord." Because of Rip, he helped open many doors for me from that point.

Rip's teachings have stuck with me since day one and that is something I have incorporated and passed on those teachings to my students here in the UK at RWA (Al Snow Wrestling Academy Cheshire.) Rip has made various trips over here to the UK to hold seminars at my schools, something I never would have dreamed would have happened years ago! He is a man who wants to give back! A man who will invest countless hours in you. He lives for this business. He has trained the worlds best!

From me personally, THANK YOU Rip for everything you have done for me. I will owe you for the rest of my life!

Andy Baker
Owner RWA Wrestling

PREFACE

Is Less More?

This is a strong polarizing topic among wrestlers, and wrestling fans at the moment. There are those that will say these teachings are old and out of date and to get with the times and that things have changed and will never go back to the way they were. Very possibly true as you can see this new age of pro wrestlers/entertainers making careers out of what they do that are on the contrary to many points mentioned here. On the other side, never was wrestling more popular, made more money, and offered more jobs to wrestlers than back in "the old" days where most, if not all of these points were held as standard. The most successful in our industry, (The Rock, Stone Cold Steve Austin, Hulk Hogan, etc) followed the "old school mentality" that if wrestlers and promoters did more of, business would likely grow for all.

Even if you disagree with the majority of what is written here. Of all the topics covered, of everything that is mentioned, I believe it is almost certain that you will still find something valuable in the pages to come.

When you start out on your path of becoming a pro wrestler, you will learn that there is more to this business than you could ever imagine. You will make plenty of mistakes, hopefully learning from them all as you progress. One of the fastest ways to learn this business is going into it with the right attitude. But what does that really mean? The following pages will tell you.

What is written here is not meant to be read through in one sitting. These points need to be thoroughly considered and properly applied to really stick with you. You will need to go back and re read this book and the points that stick out to you many times. Use a highlighter, bookmarks, or circle the points that really stand out to you so that you can easily come back to them and refresh your memory.

Rip Rogers

Mark Sciarra, born in Seymour, Indiana February 7th 1954 better known by his ring name Rip Rogers, has been involved in the pro wrestling business in one form or another for over 40 years. Rogers has travelled all over the world, wrestling for countless wrestling promotions from Durbin, South Africa, The Maritime Provinces, Puerto Rico, Japan, all across the US, and more. When you think of any big name wrestlers from past or present, Rip has likely either been in the ring with them, or worked with them some way or another. To this day, you will see many of the current top stars in the business acknowledging the lessons they've learned from Rogers.

Rip Rogers is currently head trainer at OVW (Ohio Valley Wrestling). Anyone who has ever had a chance to be part of Rip's training class or seminars has been fortunate enough to learn from one of the all time greats. The stories alone that Rip has could be a book in and of itself.

Some of the biggest names in wrestling today have also gone through Rip's courses at OVW. Randy Orton, Brock Lesnar, Dave Batista, and John Cena included. 64 people (and counting) have earned jobs with either WWE, Impact

Wrestling, and ROH while training at OVW with Rip. This number does not include people that were scouted previously and then sent to Rip for training, but people who came to OVW on their own accord with a dream of making it in the business. Notable figures include, JTG and Shad Gaspard Cryme Tyme, Armando Estrada, Serena Deeb, Mike Mondo (Spirit Squad), Nick Dinsmore (Eugene), Rob Conway, Santino Marella, and Anarquia, just to name a few.

In addition to wrestling and coaching, Rip has also competed in and won bodybuilding competitions and pro boxing matches.

Rip Rogers with the original "Nature Boy" Buddy Rogers.

"The Convertible Blonds"
"Pistol" Pez Whatley   "Hustler" Rip Rogers

Attitude

Always enjoy the journey on your way to making it. Money, fame, prestige, are great, but the friends you make, the things you experienced on your journey looking back, will be the highlight of your life. Take it all in. Bad and good. Remember.

Always remember the ones that really helped you understand this business, and return the favor if you're ever in a position to.

When breaking in for Dick the Bruiser I was hardly ever booked, but made the towns. I got there early, helped with anything they wanted. Always dressed out whether I was booked or not. I shut up and tried to learn. Soon I was getting booked more and Dick Bruiser booked me other places.

Blessings usually come in wrestling after you selflessly give of yourself to help others. You always have a special bond to those that helped you.

Ricky Morton was a pleasure to work with because instead of worrying about getting his shit in, he was more concerned selling his heel and the match.

Don't ever think you're bigger than the sport. It was fine before you and will be just as fine when you quit. Pass on the knowledge.

You should put the same effort in a match at the flea market as you would Wrestle Mania. Prep, psychology, intensity, be a real pro.

Asked to put someone over and you pout? Don't be a dick! Do it right! If you can't lose correctly you will not be trusted to win correctly. If you're booked to lose, please do it to the best of your ability. Do as the boss wants. If all did this, we would all make more money. Everyone should learn to lose properly before they ever learn to win properly. It's not real when you win nor is it real when you lose. Nothing like watching a guy when he learns he's supposed to lose. Read that body language. Is he all in for it or is he a prick? The wrestling business is not real. You're not really a champ or a loser. That's your role. Play that role of the loser the best you can and some day you will be champ.

Nobody is bigger than pro wrestling. It will survive nicely without you. Keep a great attitude, do it the right way and help the newbies

When the boys think they are too good to practice, it's the beginning of them turning into cancer. Bad attitudes, knowing it all, it's a pattern.

To new young wrestlers in the business; this is a complicated business with mental aspect really more important than the physical. Stay humble, attitude is everything. Stay away from negativity. This is a very "Me, me," business. Beware. Many start, few last.

Everybody wants to work somebody with a great attitude that will do his best to get the match over. Nobody wants to work with an asshole that is strictly out to put himself over.

Be good to the wrestling business and it will be good to you. Might take awhile, but hang in there, do it right, and you will be rewarded. The wrestling business is a marathon, not a sprint. It's how you finish the race, not how you start.

Always remember the ones that really helped you understand this business. Return the favor if you are ever in a position to do so.

Without the ref, time keeper, announcer, ring jacket boys, ring crew, ticket taker, ushers, security, it's hard to have a show. Respect everybody. We are all part of this thing called pro wrestling, and it's wonderful.

Never consider yourself "too good" to do what is asked of you. Nobody is bigger than the sport. Remember how badly you just wanted to be accepted by the other performers. Attitude and humility will take you far.

You will still be learning till the day you die. What to do or what not to do. You think you already know it all, is the start of your demise.

Treat this business with respect, work hard, do as asked to the best of your ability. Help others with less experience. Respect all involved.

Do the finish as the boss tells you. Have same positive attitude whether you are squashing your foe or getting squashed. Attitude is everything.

Having confidence in yourself is one thing, thinking you are better than someone else is another.

Any school, college, trade school, costs money. You want to be a wrestler but complain about the price? Tell that to law or med school.

The most important attribute you can have in your quest to be a pro wrestler is ATTITUDE. A bad one can destroy you while a good one makes you.

I've seen guys actually get mad because they are told to lose a match. Boys feel free to apply at McDonald's.

Learn as many aspects of wrestling as you can and perform them to 100% of your ability . A great positive attitude is contagious.

How anybody in wrestling can have an ego is beyond me. When you win, it's not real. When you lose, its not real. You're just playing a role.

If I was the boss and somebody didn't like a finish, I would be wishing them good luck in their future endeavors.

In any job you do as the boss wants. It's his company. Don't like it? Get a new job or start your own company. If you're good, your time will come.

Rip Rogers and the late Owen Hart.

p Rogers and William Regal.

As you begin training and start experiencing the early stage of what it's like to be a pro wrestler, you will be sore, tired, and a myriad of other emotions that will likely make you want to give up. Whether you started wrestling for fun or because you want to make this your career, you will need a motivational boost to keep you on your path. Seek out the stories of others who "made it" and you will find that many of them had situations much more difficult than you could ever imagine.

Motivation

Some people make an excuse for everything, but the ones that succeed, overcome every barrier placed in front of them.

Everybody at WWE were once fans like you were. Somehow they found a way to make it. Probably called never giving up while others laughed.

You can't teach drive, determination, and desire. Some have it, but most don't. Those that do are special, and will make it.

We chose to be in the wrestling business. It didn't choose us. Stop bitching and get your ass in gear to be the best you can be at all aspects of it.

When you get a chance to carry the ball, you better be ready. You waited your whole life for this. Time for a touchdown!

You can never be too good a wrestler, in too good of shape, too good at promos, have too good of costumes, outwork them all. Be your very best.

Michael Jordan got cut from his high school basketball team. Dennis Rodman made NBA roster at about 26 and Scottie pippin started out as a manager of a basketball team in college, so don't give up.

WWE always has their eye on Impact, ROH, NJPW, and others all over the world no matter what they tell you. Get great and they will find you.

Almost every star I know almost quit because of financial hardships, stress on loved ones, too much emotional bullshit, but didn't.

Take your weaknesses and make them your strengths. Leave no stone unturned in your quest to be the best you can be in your dream.

It's better to go after your passion 100% and not make it, than to go through your life wondering if you could have. Passion keeps you alive.

The road to being a pro wrestling star is very tough. You will suffer setback after setback. You will be mocked and made fun of by your family and friends. You will be broke and in debt. You must train, diet, and practice daily to even have a chance. You in or out?

Most green horns give up. This is a very hard business. If you stay the course, stay positive, and surround yourself with good people, the light bulb will eventually go off in your head and you will get this. But you gotta gut it out!

For those chasing a dream; remember how long it took WWE to sign Finn Baylor, Kevin Owens, AJ Styles, Cesaro, etc, don't give up your dream.

I never knew any wrestler that wasn't ridiculed for his career choice, until he made it.

Wrestling is like HS football, first day 65 are there, 2nd day 44, third day 32, There's your team. The rest can't cut it.

Hopefully pro wrestling keeps you humble and the little boy in you that admired your heroes. You're probably somebody's hero yourself. Remember that always.

Even if you never make a dime, the experience, the adventures, the stories, the friendships you make in your quest to be a pro are life lessons.

Now is the time to push harder, train harder, practice more, go nuts on promos and strikes. Nobody was ever disappointed giving 100%

If anybody tries to talk you out of your dream tell them to fuck off. Just because they settled, doesn't mean you should. Go get your dream.

Every major star has a unique story all his own. Believe me, they wanted to give up too at some point, but didn't.

Everybody that's a star today was once in your shoes. Copying the stars and dreaming of being there themselves. All of them.

You only have so much time in your lifetime. Whatever you want, go get it before it's too late. If you don't, you will regret it the rest of your life.

Nobody said life was fair. Don't give up no matter what. Chase that dream until its yours. Let nothing stop you.

To be in WWE you are chasing a long shot, but so were the guys you now idolize on TV. It took them many years to get there but they didn't give up. Will you?

Nobody said life was fair. If you're a wrestlers kid, ex pro athlete, related, know big wig, reality star, you have an advantage. If not, WORK HARD.

If you continually improve in all aspects of wrestling and you keep knocking on the door you will get there. Ask Viktor (Ascension).

Every Wrestler in WWE has a very different and unique story to tell how they fought and clawed their way to their goal. Never giving up and beating the odds. Every one, a different journey to get there. Different hardships and sacrifices to make it. But in the end they are smiling. They did the impossible.

Dreaming to be a pro wrestler? Dreaming isn't going to get it. You will go to class, diet, train, like a nut, and suffer immensely before you make it.

If you get a chance to get in a ring tomorrow and practice, remember how at one time you just wanted a chance, just a chance to get in there.

I'm not into excuses. Show up early, every class. Work hard. Push to be great. Eat right, train, repeat every day you're alive.

Wrestling is a grind. Every day diet, gym, trips, hard work, but a labor of love if it's your passion. If it's not, you will soon quit.

Don't judge a book by its cover. Most stars were told "No, no, no." For years. They didn't give up. Ask Owens, Finn, Cesaro, it isn't easy.

You know you're starting to make it when people start knocking you. They are mad because they gave up and you're still going after your dream despite setbacks.

Choices in life: drink, smoke, do drugs, break the law, do steroids, work hard, be a role model. It's all up to us, nobody else.

You have one life, please do what the hell you want to do no matter what anybody else says. If you don't, you will be mad at yourself forever.

You should be waking up every day chomping at the bit to get better at each aspect of wrestling. This is on you to push yourself and get things done.

Don't feel bad, everybody was the shits at pro wrestling when they started. You will get better. Keep pushing. The moves are the easy part. Trying to understand the psychology part of wrestling is the hard part. Eventually you will get it and will be an excellent story teller.

When you don't like your finish, didn't get your shit in, had to carry a green guy, bitched about your payoff or long trip, remember how you dreamed of being a pro wrestler and would do anything to reach your goal. You wanted in. Attitude is everything.

Learn to embrace the grind. Every day is another day to push yourself to get better at the business you chose to be in.

If you're not practicing your sport and giving it 100% someone who is will get that job that you half assed. You can't teach drive, you got it or you don't.

Stop making excuses and get it done. There's 24 hours a day for all. Get your ass up and do what you gotta do to make it. Champs do, losers don't.

Dreams don't come true without a lot of work, heartbreak, suffering, and setbacks. But if you do the work, don't give up, that dream is your reality.

Everybody at WWE were once fans like you. Somehow they found a way to make it. Probably called never giving up while others laughed.

Only you can do the work. Only you can do what needs to be done. Only you are responsible for your actions. Nobody else can make you. It's up to you.

Whatever role or job your given in wrestling, give it 100%. You're in the business you love. Chase that dream.

When you're broke, work your ass off to be noticed. When you get signed, work harder to make the main roster. When you make it, keep the pedal to the metal.

Years from now when your filthy rich and over world wide, you will think of all hardships you endured. The laughs and crying, and you will realize it's the journey of giving your all to make it that is the gratification.

Most everybody in WWE has a unique story with trials and tribulations of just hanging on to get that dream. So don't give up, don't ever give up. God put you on this earth to be a pro wrestler and you will be.

Nobody but you is keeping you from being the best you can be. Drive, determination, and dedication determines your destination.

Patience. Quite the virtue. Keep grinding towards your goal. Devote 100% to it knowing you will suffer setbacks and rejection, and more obstacles. Hang in there. What you pursue will eventually be yours. Patience.

It takes someone very special to make it. The ups and downs drive a normal person crazy. Without a good support system, it's even harder to succeed. But certain people keep working no matter what. And they be the ones that make it.

Pro wrestling, it's a long, long, journey. Learn from both the highs and the lows but always keep pushing towards your goal. Work hard, stay positive, be consistent, enjoy the ride of the world's greatest sport. Pro rasslin.

Always give 100% in every match. Mentally, physically, and emotionally. Always remember how you felt as a kid going to the matches. Your match may inspire many to chase a dream and be like you. Who inspired you?

No matter what you want, no matter what you desire, keep working towards that goal to get it. Without that goal, without that desire, a man is virtually dead. Goals keep us alive. Keep plugging.

Don't get mad at me or anyone else because you half ass it. You got one life, one dream, one passion. Takes 100%

effort until you get there. Then you work even harder to stay there. This is on you. Own it. Get that dream, no excuses.

Whatever your dream is, go get it. Quit waiting and stop making excuses. There's never a perfect time to start. Just get your ass in gear. Go get the damn dream!

The more you experience setbacks and obstacles, the smarter you become. The more mistakes you make, the more you really understand it, and when you finally make it, and you will, you will have a finer appreciation of attaining your goal and can look back with pride.

Give me that guy with passion for pro wrestling. Not some super athlete. The super athlete just wants the paycheck. The passionate one hardly thinks about the money. He just wants to be a wrestler. A great one too.

Been training guys at OVW for 20 years. 64 have earned jobs with WWE, Ring of Honor, Impact, as wrestlers, refs, office people, announcers, etc. These were people who walked in and paid with their own dime. Not contract people. Find your passion and don't let go.

When you're trying to be signed to WWE, think of it this way, act like you want to be a Dr. Go to college 4 years, 3 years medical school, internship, etc. You're investing in yourself. You'll be in debt and still a rookie Dr. It isn't easy. Chase that dream.

You work, you dream, you train, you diet, you sacrifice, you travel, you face financial crisis, relationship troubles, you feel shit on. You're mad, but your one step closer to the day you will make it, and you will keep on until you do.

Guys don't get it. You're trying to make it to WWE. The number one pro wrestling company in the world. There are tens of thousands others wanting it too. You can't fucking half ass it! You gotta push yourself to be the best you can be in all aspects of the business

Your goal might take ten years or more to achieve, with obstacles and heartbreak guaranteed. You will get it in the end. Believe in yourself.

Some guys give it 100% and bust their ass to make it to NBA. Some are happy playing church league. Wrestling is the same way. Which one are you?

If you keep working hard, don't give up, keep learning, keep improving, you will eventually get a shot Show those who doubted you that you are a star.

Believe in yourself! If you don't, how in the hell do you expect anybody else to? Know your craft inside and out! Be the best you can be.

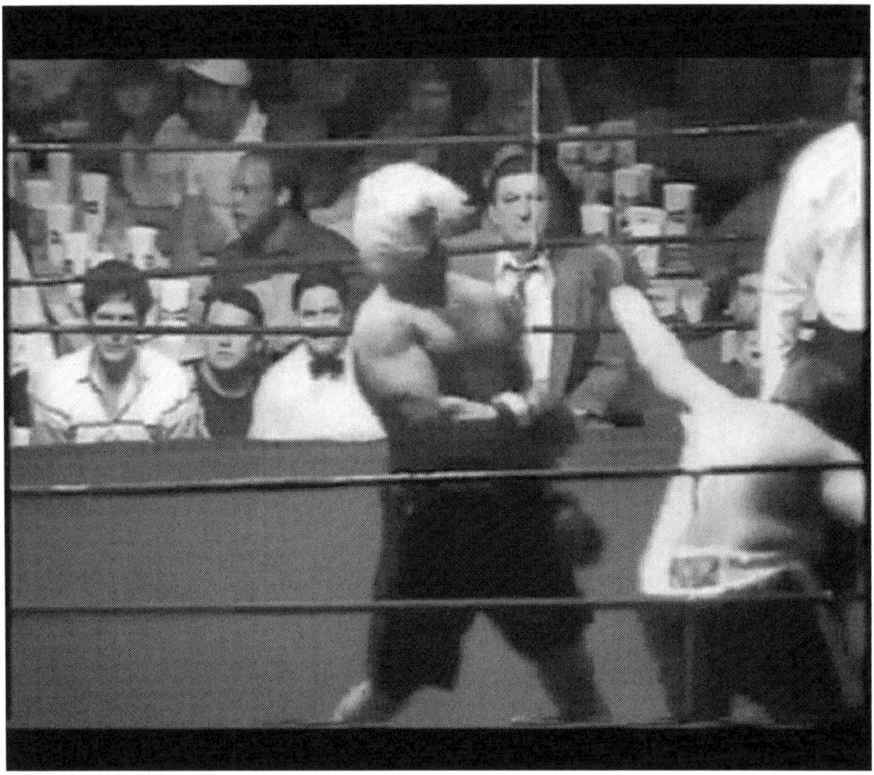

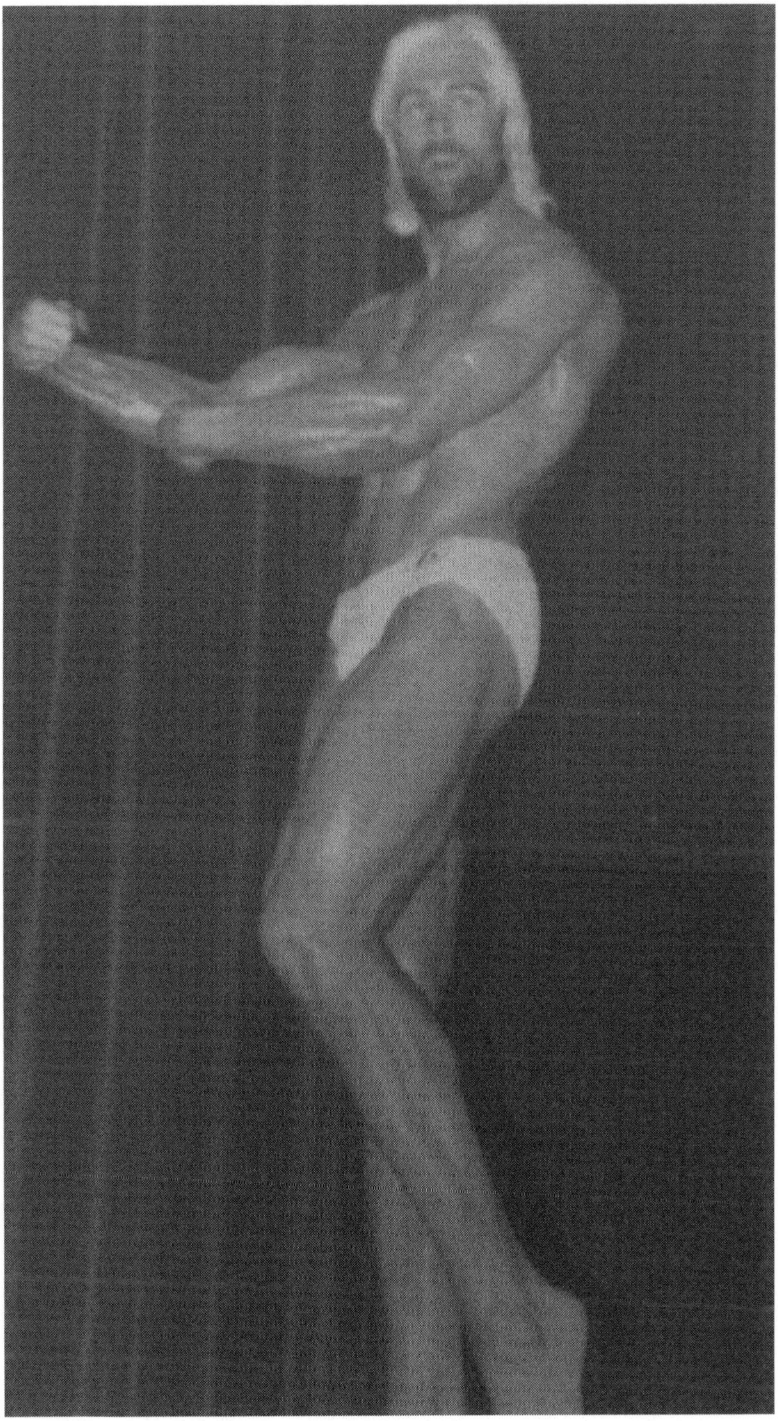

Selling

Selling is a lost art in today's wrestling. The more you sell your opponent the more your comeback will mean. Simple but effective.

Selling each other correctly makes the match so much easier and believable. A big move with no selling renders the move irrelevant. The better you sell, the less you need to do and the more everything means.

When selling, keep your head up so everyone in the audience can see your facials. Your whole body language should mirror your facials. A 5 year old child should understand.

The art of selling sets you apart from the others. The scouts know that you know. It's not the bump, but the selling of it.

Big dangerous moves with minimal selling means nothing. Sell any move like it's real and you will make fans believe and make your match so much easier.

You want your match to get over and be different? Simple, sell each other. Give us basics with fire, emotion, and intensity. Make it look like you hate each other. Like a junior high fight. Make them believe, and sell.

The bumps you do at 25 you begin to feel at 40. How I wish I would have sold the bump correctly so I didn't need any more.

You only have so many bumps on your bump card. When it's used up, you're done. Don't waste them. Learn to get max mileage out of them.

Instead of taking ten bumps, take one and get all the mileage you can out of it. Your body language should tell every fan there what's hurting.

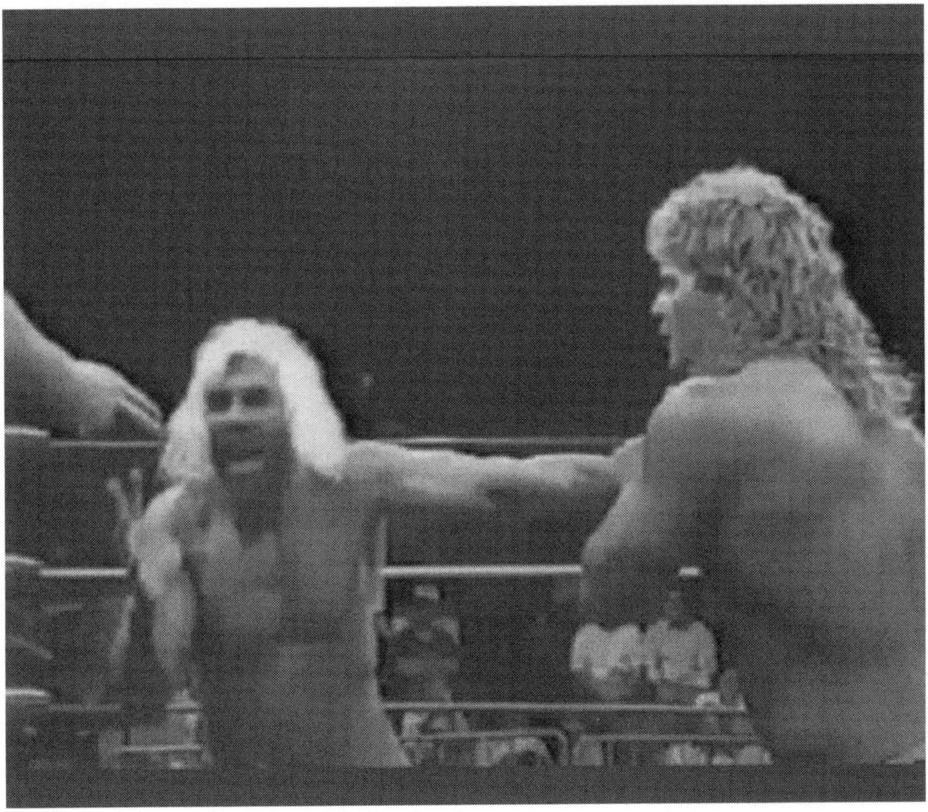

Faces

As a face learn how and when to register and sell. How to fight back without dying, how to stay alive but staying the underdog.

Verne Gagne was always a face. I think Ricky steamboat too. Fans believed in them.

Faces please let the heels throw the first punch, chop, strike, or kick. They are supposed to be the bad guy. If u do it first, you're the bad guy.

Don't be afraid to put that heel over strong if you're winning the match. Nothing like a come from behind win in any sport.

If you're a face winning, let the heel dominate and beat you up to get sympathy. In the end David will beat Goliath. That's all that matters.

If you're a face, do a spot with a 3 part rhythm. On the last move (example slam) act like you tweak your knee. Register, turn to the right, and have foe clip you. Heat.

Please don't feed your hurt body part to a heel if he's getting heat on it. Treat it like you're really hurt. Keep it away, make him earn it.

If the heel is getting heat on your left arm, protect it like it's really hurt. Make him really work to attack it. You know he's after it, the fans know it too, so make him earn it. He might punch you in the jaw since your focused on protecting your arm, but then he's on it while you sell the punch. Make him earn his heat. Make it believable. It's a contest, tell a story.

A comeback should be retribution on what the heel did to you. Just like in the movies. If the heel hit you with the kendo stick 5 times, what should you do when he drops it? Three clotheslines? Ten super kicks? Or pick that stick up and beat the hell out of him?

A comeback in wrestling is like the movies. What the heel did to face, he gives back to heel as revenge. Plus one. Simple.

Don't start a comeback, then do a reversal. It causes a dip in your rhythm and hurts your build. Comeback is all you baby! No dips, you just kick ass!

As a face never let a heel kick out of a big move, but have him get his foot over bottom rope to stop the count. Keep yourself looking strong.

If you're a good guy and you turn to the ref and hold up your fingers in a 2 sign after a kick out,1. You come across like a complainer. 2. You make yourself look like a divvy because you'd know if it was 3 as the bell would of rung. A villain can complain. Think!

As a face don't promise the fans you're going to win. You might not. But do promise to give 100%.

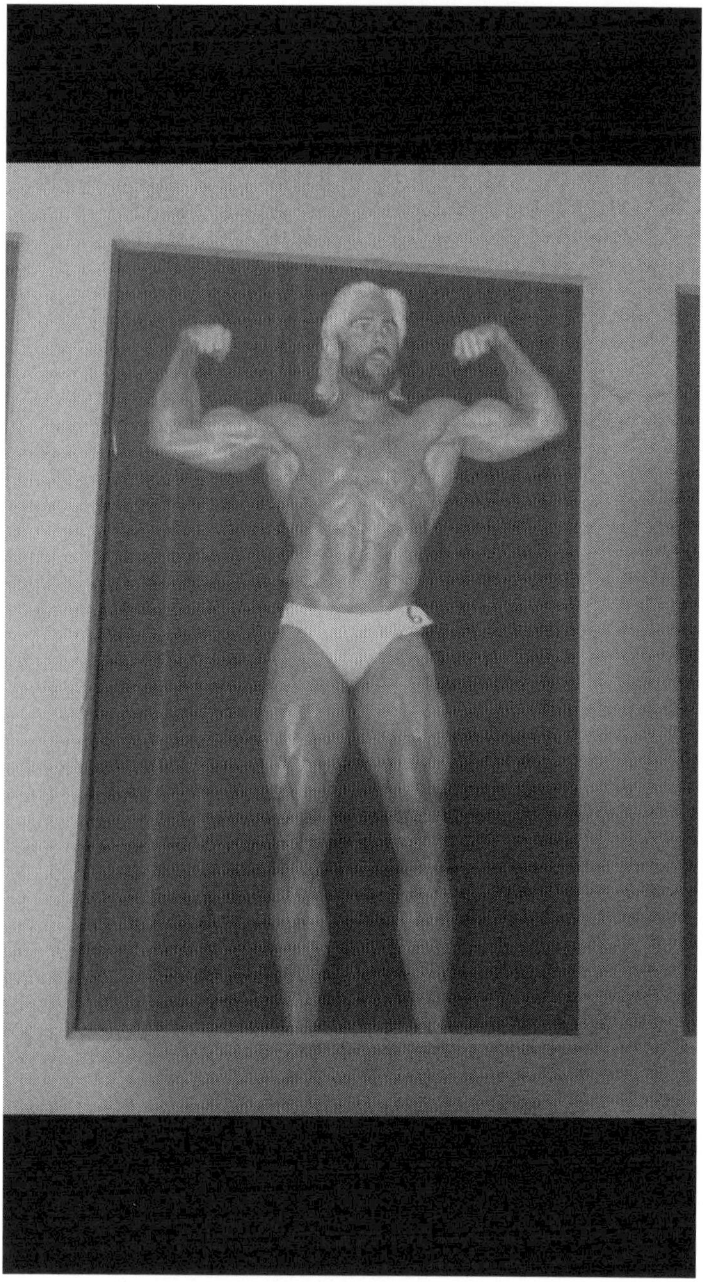

Rip Rogers and Macho Man Randy Savage

Heels

As a heel, look like you could kick somebody's ass. Use exaggerated facials and body language. Learn to use those eyes to glare a whole through those booing you. Be aggressive, make your bumps mean something, know when to register, sell, and back away.

Learn to get viscous heat on every body part using holds and strikes. Arm, leg, neck, stomach, back and learn to meat chop. Beat the shit out of them with different strikes, chops, kicks, head butts, rakes, etc. look violent.

Once you hurt the babyface's body part, everything should be isolated on it. His back is hurt, moves, strikes, holds, should be back oriented only.

Keep your heat. Be a no good bastard! Whenever you cover a face, don't let him kick out on you. Hook the tights, foot on rope, elbow on throat, ref catches you but you keep heat and your just punishing the face. Stay aggressive, especially if the face is winning. Put ref over but keep heat.

When a face wants to get all his shit in just let him. Have him cover you each time and just kick out on one. Then when it's time for heat, just stop him. You took all his shit then stopped him. He will eventually figure it out. I hope.

Make your opponent earn his comeback. No zero to hero. You kill the match. A slow believable comeback with a fitting climax is best.

If face is beating you, he doesn't need near falls. Near falls are needed when you're going to beat him. So he almost pins you till you get one on him.

Heels, if your winning don't kick out of faces pin attempt, but get your foot on the rope or grab the rope to stop the count. You're winning, make him look great.

If your'e a heel leading a match, every move, maneuver sequence, high spot, should be telling a story that the average fan can understand.

It's up to you to be the QB in the ring. Each guy has different strengths and weaknesses and it's up to you to make him the best he can be.

Watch the matches and don't repeat spots from earlier matches. Get heat on different body part, make the comeback be retribution for the heat, sell each other.

Be smart, if everybody is doing spots and coming off the top, do the opposite. It's a buffet, give them some steak instead of chicken again.

The bigger the bump as a heel, the more exaggerated your facials and body language are to get that face to connect with the audience to see him kick ass.

Keep the heat on you for being devious and not on the ref. You want fans mad at you, not him. Be a smart, evil, sneaky, SOB. You gotta draw not the ref.

A comeback by the face on the heel should be retribution on the heel by the face. Example : if he punched you 10 times, do same to him plus one.

Heels don't give it the old "Oh my god he kicked out on my big hold" face. He's winning, punish him, make it an upset, keep your heat.

A heels job is to get the marks mad so they will pay money to see the face kick his ass. Of course it might take ten shows to do it.

If you're a heel and want cheers, you should be a face. Boos and jeers to a heel, is like applause to the face. It takes a special kind to be a real heel.

Don't be afraid to be a wrestling heel. It adds to the card. It's ok to out wrestle the face in the beginning, but soon he turns the tables on you.

There's no need to line up spots. I know what you can do well. I'm a heel. I lead this show like a QB. It's on me if it's good or not.

It's ok to be a wrestling heel, but eventually the face outwrestles you and you take shortcuts to be on top. If you want cheers be a face.

Want some heat? Heel throws one cheap punch and pins face. Face oversells for 5 minutes and has to be helped back to dressing room. Heat. Simple.

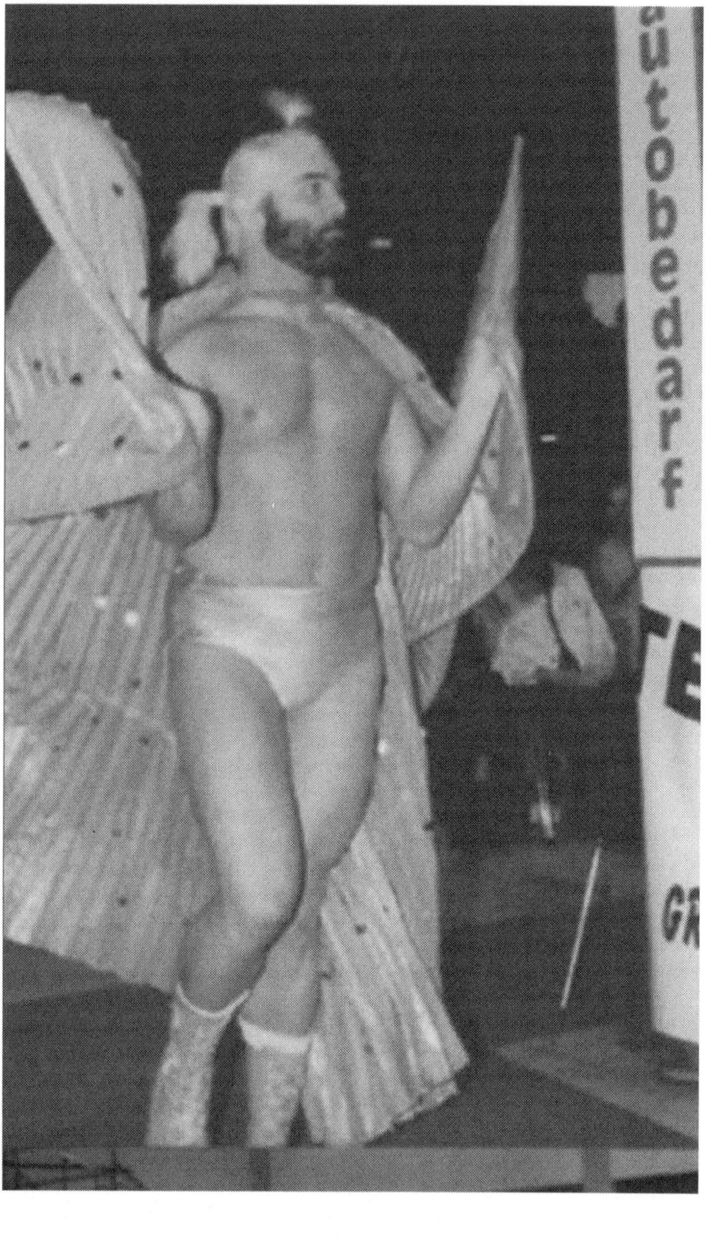
autobedarf

Tag Matches

The purpose of a tag team match is for both teams to work as a team, not two single matches. Have a lot of tags, Heel double teams, work as a unit. Heels double team first.

If your tag match is scheduled for less than 30 minutes, one heat to the best seller, usually smaller guy. Start the heat after 15 minutes after a rise spot to get seller over before he sells.

Big part of a tag team match is learning how to work the corner as a face while your partner is selling and fighting to give you the hot tag!!!!

His job is to sell and tag as he's been taking the heat, when the time is right, he then makes hot tag to fresh guy with fresh heel.

During the match, the heels will always save and go to ropes for break first. On saves, heel use strikes, face pulls off at first, but later retaliates like heel.

Faces, please don't use double team moves on the heels first. Let them be the heels.

When you're selling in a tag match the object is to get away and tag your partner because you're in real trouble. You don't need a double down or big move. Your job is to sell until you finally make the tag. Your partner is fresh and he kicks their ass. If you give them a bump before the tag, it kills your partners comeback! This simple tactic can make or break your tag match. Do it right with no ego and you will get great results.

Do one false tag (a false tag is when the faces make a legal tag but the referee is distracted so does not see it and forces the incoming partner back out of the ring) right before the hot tag to get them pissed off as much as possible. DO NOT have the guy selling do a big move then tag.

Rip Rogers and The British Bulldog Davey Boy Smith

Understanding the psychology of pro wrestling is the one of the most difficult parts of being a pro wrestler. When you start to get it, it will seem very common sense. But getting to that point takes a lot of training under the watchful eyes of someone with the right know-how who can guide you. Simply being aware of the points below will you put among a very small percentage of wrestlers in the business today. Comprehending them and being able to implement them in your matches, will you put you among the elite levels.

Psychology

The art of pro wrestling is; feigning violence as a wrestling contest, using emotion, facials, body language, good vs evil, good selling, and evil getting heat; set up by angles and promos to get maximum mileage out of anything and everything.

Guys get hurt today because they are in the ring without understanding the psychology of pro wrestling. The moves are a dime a dozen. Selling them correctly and making you believe in them is the art. This is not a stunt show, but an athletic psychological ballet.

If every tie up is smooth, if every time you try and grab a hold it's successful, then your match is too smooth. Make it a contest. Emotion!

Have some failure in trying to get a hold! Make a bump mean something. Sell each other, make a pin attempt mean something. Intensity!

You and you alone have the power to make fans believe yours is a contest and not like the rest. Show emotion! Get mad! Just like if it was real!

Dives, too many moves, excessive strikes will come and go, but the art of pro wrestling, if done correctly, will live forever. Facials, body language, emotion and intensity get an audience going every time and always will.

No matter what people are still people. Give them a good competitive match selling each other & they will buy into it. Do too much, they can see it's horse shit.

This business is not that complicated. Two competitive athletes giving their best to win. We made it complicated.

You watch UFC and you're afraid to go to the bathroom because the fight could turn and end just like that. Wrestling can do the same. Treat it like a contest.

Intensity and emotion are the keys to a good match. Sell each other correctly. Tell a story and you're looking at a potential great one.

The moves in wrestling are the easy part. It's when to use them, how, where, and why is the part that takes so long to understand.

What is a 5 star match? Too many bumps and they mean nothing. Too many strikes, ditto. Face gets his shit in and doesn't win, he's weak. Submissions held on too long makes submission skills poor.

You want to stand out? Be different. Nothing outlandish. Every match has a dive. Now it's nothing special. Instead show me some facials, body language, and intensity. Make them believe yours is a contest, and you're going to whoop his ass! Very simple.

How was your match? I got 3 dives in, my 450, my Canadian Destroyer, and all my karate kicks and 12 clotheslines. You won? Huh? No, I submitted on arm.

If you're losing and you get all your shit in, obviously all your shit ain't shit because you lost.

When you do your big moves that your opponent kicks out on, all your doing is putting him over and making you look so weak with your big cool moves. Dick the Bruiser didn't cover anyone unless it was the finish. Nobody kicks out on the Bruiser.

How can you speed up in a match if you're going fast to begin with? You can't. You have to slow down so that picking up the tempo means something.

Whoever said three clothes lines bump feed is good, is an idiot. Comeback is retribution on heel.

When you jump right up after a clothesline into two more, they mean zero. You can still do them in 3's but slow the rhythm down, let the audience digest what is happening.

Like in a movie, you have to sell before the comeback and be ultimate heel before you turn face. Now you don't know what to expect from me. But you will think, "I know that bastard is gonna turn!"

Too many false finishes especially 2 counts, make them almost irrelevant. Too much size difference the bigger one shitty if he doesn't win.

You didn't cover buddy Rogers unless you beat him or he could get his foot on the ropes. He kept covers and faces over by making any cover special.

A pin attempt should mean something. The more you have, the less they mean. Just like punches, big moves and bumps.

On the finish make sure both of your shoulders are down for the full 3 count. Don't ever hook tights or use ropes for leverage in finish unless boss tells you to. Heat goes to ref for missing it and cheapens your win.

Please get heat on a different body part each match. Faces please dominate with a different anchor each match. It's not that hard if u get it.

Rest hold? No such thing. You slam, suplex, beel, turnbuckle, backdrop, use multiple strikes on a guy's back; its hurt now. You wear it down with a hold.

There are no such things as "Rest Holds" your isolating a particular body part that has been weakened with strikes, blows, now trying to submit that part.

A face that really sells correctly makes the match so so easy. Too many want to stay strong. Everybody loves the underdog. Heels that want to do cool moves and want cheers need to be a baby face. It's not that complicated.

Faces if you're going over, don't be afraid to sell really well for the heel because in the end you're going to win. Heel, if you're winning the match, make that face look as great as possible. In the end you're going over.

Don't try and reinvent the wheel. If you're losing in a competitive match, take more. If you're winning, sell more. Nothing like the home team or face coming from behind to win.

The more they hated you as a heel, the more they will love you as a face. And vice versa.

You don't counter a move first, you set the tone by delivering the move once at least, twice is better; example. Slam, slam, small package.

The best finish hold for you is one that can be used on anyone from Andre to Sky Low Low, with no chance of you or them getting hurt. Just make sure it cops a pin or submission. Nobody kicks out of it or it isn't a finish. If it's not the finish, don't use it. Simple.

Hardest things in wrestling biz to master are a good looking, working punch that barely touches you. Learning to sell properly, learning to slow down and not doing too much in your match.

Too many punches with no marks or swelling means you can't punch. Limit them to face and oversell them. Treat a punch as a real punch.

Protect your strikes. Make sure they are sold properly. If not then don't throw them or throw real ones. That always seems to make them sell.

Treat your punch as a real one. Don't give him 3 then have him reverse your whip, you just killed your own punch.

Don't throw too many punches no matter how good they look. If you hit a guy 20 times and there's not a mark on him, you just killed yourself.

The threat of hitting someone with a chair, closed fist, gimmick, knucks, is so much more dramatic than the actual act. The threat.

It's not the punch, it's the threat of it. It's not the chair, the gimmick, the piledriver, etc, it's the emotion of "Oh no, here it comes!"

When in doubt, grab a headlock. Sell it. Every kid 5 and up knows what it is. Most fights everywhere, that's what they go for.

If a guy is not a high spot man, don't do them. Highlight strengths, hide weaknesses. Make him look as good as he can be.

Want to make your match easier? Heels be heels, faces sell heels, heels back up, bump, and beg on comeback. Book backwards to maximize finish.

Don't poke a guy in the eyes and then do a high spot. Don't hurt a guy's leg and then give turnbuckle or throw into ropes. Fall down in pain.

Don't ever do an eye rake, then do a high spot. A poke in the eye is definitely starting your heat.

Don't call your opponent fat, skinny, young, or old. If you won, who did u beat?

Don't be doing shit just for the sake of doing it. Takes time to learn how, what, when, where, and why if at all.

HTM cud get more heat and mileage just threatening to take a bump than most guys today. He understood the art of selling and less is more.

Force yourself to learn to call it in the ring. That's how you get good. Don't go in with pre planned bullshit. You're the QB, call it on the fly.

Every match is not supposed to be the main event. Not every hitter is cleanup hitter, shooting guard or QB. Learn to work your slot correctly.

If face gives DDT to heel, either heel rolls to floor or is by rope to get his foot on the rope so you protect the DDT as a possible finisher. Protect the DDT. Stop killing the DDT. If a heel gives it to face, he can roll to floor, heel can cover and put feet on the ropes or pull tights and the ref catches him.

If as a heel I give you a big move, I will put my feet on the ropes or hook the tights, etc, so ref catches me and keeps hold good by not kicking out.

Don't put a submission hold on too long or you kill the hold. Face, put it on where heel can make the ropes.

Years ago you would have a double knockout in one match, the main event. It was kept special. You wanted fans screaming at the end of the show.

In a double knockout situation, the heel gets up first to make the face more of the underdog.

No No's in wrestling: Stop feeding your hand to the guy who's going to throw you into the ropes or buckle. Put it behind you. If you have to, make him grab it.

If you're going to do a finish that puts heat on the ref, make sure he catches you cheating every time to get him over before the dirty deed. Use your head.

A false finish gets more reaction when the move your countering has already been successful in an earlier match. Suplex, pin, suplex package pin.

False finishes mean more when you counter moves that were used as a finisher earlier. Watch other matches.

Matches are not supposed to be the same. A finisher is not a finisher unless it beats you. False finishes mean little if there are too many.

Dive should be at climax. Should cause one to be counted out. Both be counted out.

Dive is so spectacular, you can't follow it with anything. Make it mean something. It's a main event spectacular move. Treat it as such.

"Even though I'm winning, I need to get in all my shit so I can be over." Sorry asshole you're winning, you're fighting from underneath tonight.

Snuka says "Brudda, finish is splash. Just beat me up till comeback and finish."

If there's going to be some heat on the ref at the finish, make sure he is super ref, and catches you trying to cheat every time until the end.

Please, please, don't really pull the guy over on a sunset flip. Let him milk, sell, pantomime, and he will go down when he's ready.

There is nothing worse than a diva with an 8 inch arm clotheslining other girls. Play to your strengths girls.

If your going to miss a splash, elbow, leg drop, diving head butt, make sure if the guy doesn't move you would be on target. Nothing worse than that.

When executing a defensive pin small package off a vertical suplex attempt, let the heel get you at least a foot high off the mat until you counter.

All defensive pin attempts should be in the middle of the ring unless you want the heel to get his foot on the rope, but that kills his heat.

You have rules like no piledrivers, no over the top, nothing off top turnbuckle, no punching with closed fist, to make it seem more dangerous. Then when heel does it, you treat it as such. Without rules you cannot cheat. Can't cheat makes it harder for heel to get heat.

English wrestlers use lifters or European uppercuts because it's against the rules to throw a punch with closed fist in WOS (World Of Sport) rules. WWE needs rules.

If you're going to use superman punch as finish, don't throw any right hands resembling a punch during the match till the finish.

As a face, work a simple finish. Let's say suplex, you lose. Now stay down like you're really hurt and listen to the crowd. Milk it. Have other faces and promoter come out to see if you're ok. Simple. You got your opponent over, fans think you're really hurt and really applaud you.

Remember the threat of Kamala , King Kong Bundy, or Andre milking and almost taking a bump? When they finally went down the place exploded.

Like any sport you find your opponent's Achilles heel and keep going to it until he finally counters it. Then you change your attack. Psychology.

If your'e getting heat on a leg please don't throw a guy into turnbuckle or into the ropes. If you attempt to, have him fall down and sell his leg.

Watch any Fit Finlay match. He is always in control. The face is always the underdog. How simple is that? Easy recipe, always works.

Don't bury the ref in your match. The heat goes on him and not you. Learn distraction, rule enforcement, to get heat. Keep heat on you.

If the first three match finishes were package, sunset, back slide, use them as false finish because they already worked for the pin once.

A comeback by the face on the heel should be retribution on the heel by the face. Example: if he punched you 10 times, do same to him plus one.

The moves in wrestling are the easy part. It's when to use them, how, where, and why is the part that takes so long to understand.

Rip Rogers and Lex Luger, WCW

If you've read, understand, and can implement what you have read so far, then this next portion of the book will become or may have already become, a very likely possibility for you. Having an insight into this process will help you tremendously and could be the difference on whether you are signed by the WWE or not. Thousands of people who work years for this opportunity will never get it. If you are among the lucky ones who do, you may only get one chance at this. Make the most of it and leave no regrets.

WWE

You are always on the WWE radar. They know if you're working, if your attitude is positive or negative. When they call they will say "Be here Monday." Not 3 months from now.

When your time comes it's up to you to be ready. No advanced notice. Be tan, shaved, good gear, well groomed, in shape, adapt at promos, wrestling, humble. Be ready to attack your chance like a madman. Be polite, wear a suit, then go from Clark Kent to Superman before their very eyes.

I tell you every day to practice your promos. Now WWE wants to look at you and your panicking. Saying you're going to practice promos. Too late now.

If you're any good at all, WWE will find you. They have many scouts on the lookout for fresh talent. You never know who is watching. Be ready.

You won't be working for WWE if you're damaged goods. They want wrestlers who are healthy. Don't get injured doing dangerous shit for no money.

I hope you realize that when WWE is interested in you, you go through physicals with their doctors to see how beat up your body is. Don't be damaged goods.

When you get your WWE tryout, I bet you will wish you gave 100% in preparation for this instead of half assing it. "Wish I worked harder in class."

Do you realize what an honor it is to get a WWE tryout? Thousands wish they had a chance. Now you wish you had trained, diet, practiced promos, etc,

Your competition in WWE is like that of most sports. If you're a giant your competition is other giants. If you're a flyer, you're competition is more flyers. If you're a brawler you don't have to worry about a chain wrestling specialist. Spot monkeys your competition is other SM's. Lucha, your competition is lucha.

Then you have your ethnic groups which nobody wants to talk about. How many of each are on the roster? Like NFL, can't have 5 QB's on the team. If you're Hispanic your competition is same. Black, ditto. Englishman, German, Indian, Oriental.

Invest in yourself. Get your name out there. If not, you will be in the same place ten years from now. WWE knows those that do. You're on their list. You will be labeled an idiot by your friends and family, but this is your dream, not theirs. Fuck'em.

If you go to an established school and train under a coach who has been there, eat healthy, workout, get good gear, practice on your own, promos, punches, chaining, go to different seminars, you have a good chance to get a WWE tryout. You don't. You probably won't.

To make it in WWE it's pretty much mandatory to give 100%. Once you get there, it's time to work even harder. Because now you have a bullseye on your chest. Everybody wants your spot. To make it and stay in this business takes unbelievable work ethic and dedication.

Always remember, no matter how good you are now, you started out the shits like everybody else. We get better by making mistakes but learning the solutions. So when I'm on your ass, remember I was much shittier than you!

Help each other. Forget jealousy. Do it right. Know your roll and place on the card. Do what is asked to the best of your ability. Watch the matches before you and know what main is doing so you won't step on their toes. Sell each other. Love your biz!

You can be a great worker, but unless you're on WWE TV, nobody knows about you except a select few. Get on their TV for an extended period of time and you will be looked upon as a TV star forever. Ask the legendary HTM. Still booked!

WWE is not looking for a copy of HBK, Taker. Jake, Stone Cold, The Rock, Savage, Hogan, Piper, etc, they are looking for new stars, new gimmicks.

Fact is, if you get a WWE run, you will make more money and be set for conventions and indies for next 20 years. Travel, fame, and many other perks. It's your opportunity.

In WWE some get strike one you're out forever. Some get multiple strikes and still there. If you get in, you better get zero strikes.

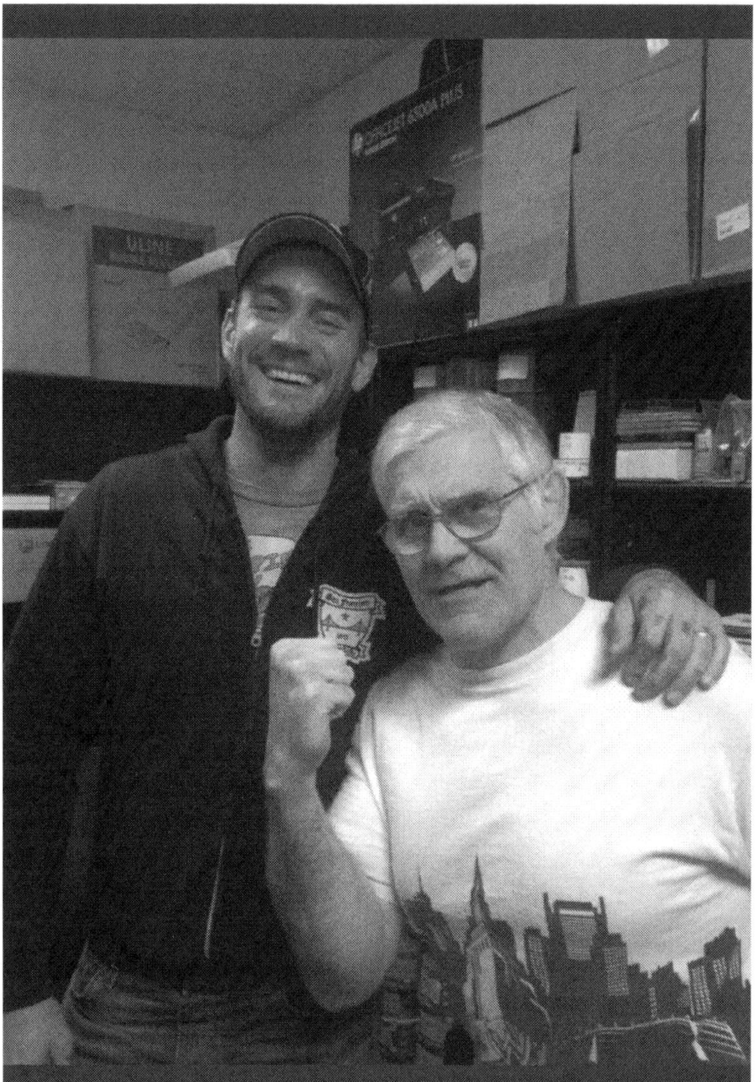

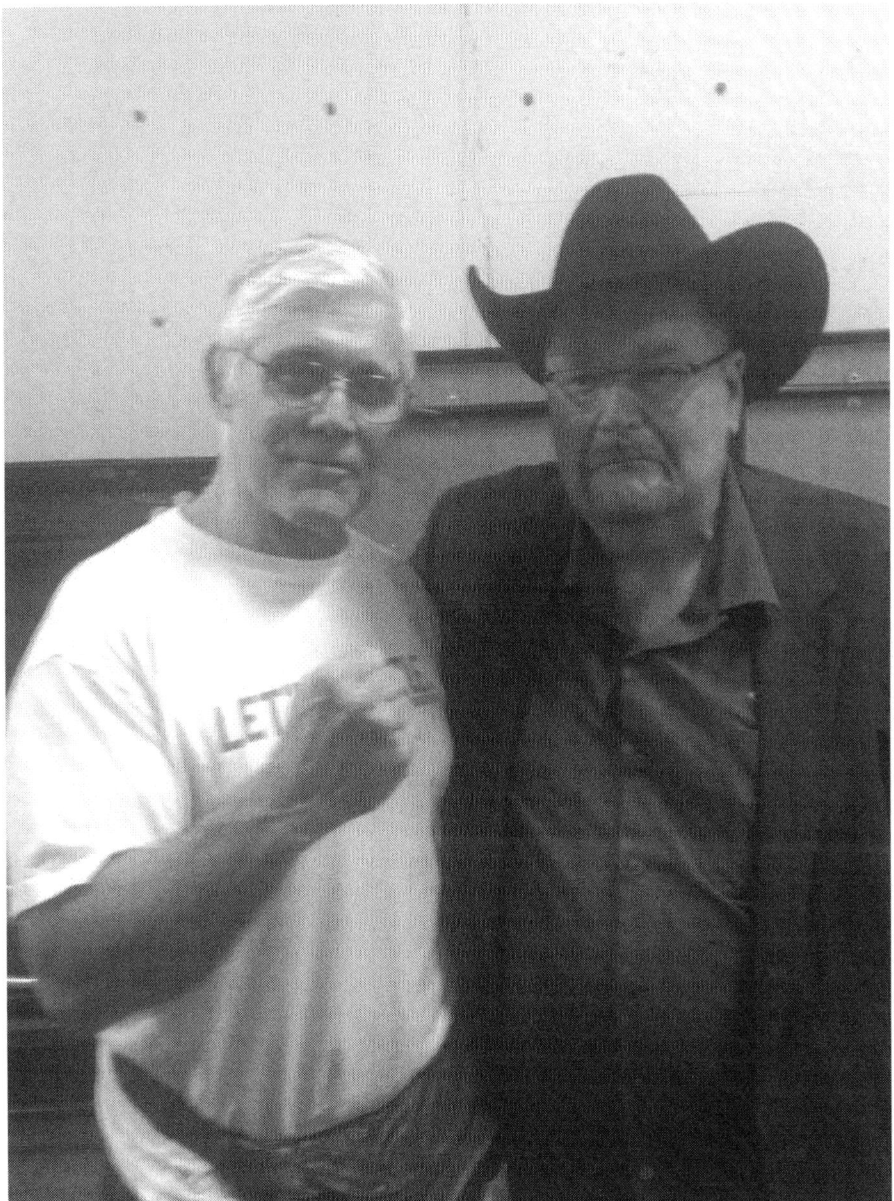

The next section of this book will be a series of random tips about many different aspects of pro wrestling. They do not fall under any one category but are invaluable none the less. Refer to these often until they are engrained in your mind.

Rip's Tip's

If you did nothing to reach your dream today, then shame on you. Somebody else got better today. You didn't. Too bad.

As a trainer I can't make you want to be the best, that's on you. Only about 1% really put the necessary work in to excel in all the basics, ring psychology, and calling it in the ring. Anybody can say they want it. Now show me you really do.

You chose to be in the wrestling business. It didn't choose you. If you're not prepared to suffer heartbreak, disappointment, obstacles and deceit, you better fold your tent now. Because it takes a tough SOB to make it in this so called business.

Reality : like all businesses in the real world, pro wrestling has nepotism, jealousy, back stabbing, lying, cheating, and every vice known to man. But no matter what it's my passion, and I will love it till I die!

You have one life, one dream, but only one body too. Don't waste your bumps unless you're really getting paid. You only got so many bumps on your bump card. Sell more, it's a lot easier to do that and get more reaction. Use your brain.

You can't play any sport at a high level without practice. You're fooling yourself if you think you can. Practice is where you work on your weakness' to make them your strengths. Games and performances are won in practice.

We don't need to reinvent the wheel. It works just fine. We need to remember though how it works, why it works, and when to use it for maximum results.

Look in the mirror. It doesn't lie. Do you look like something special? If not, do something about it. Your chances are better to make it looking great. You want to see a fat or skinny stripper or one with a great body? Hmmm...

The longer you stay in the business, the more you realize how little you knew when you thought you knew it all.

Practice all out, like your trying to make the team. Even if you're the star, you will play in the game the way you practice. There's no turning it on and off. Push to be the best you can be.

If you're being overlooked, eat better, train more, get in the ring as much as possible, practice promos and punches as much as you can. Get there early, leave late, help others. Soon you won't be overlooked.

I know movies aren't real, I go to be entertained. I don't say the movie star is overrated, this should be the finish, etc.

Fans today know wrestling isn't real, but I knew Rocky wasn't real in the theater but I still screamed for him as he made the comeback vs Apollo Creed.

Greenhorns, don't worry about cool moves, your entrance music, your big finisher, your character. First learn to wrestle, wrestle, wrestle.

You're an athletic actor, just playing a role. Have the time of your life with it. It's all a rib. Be as over the top as you can. Have fun.

Whatever needs to be done to put your opponent over, playing to what he does well, and concealing what he can't do. Intensity and aggression

No matter how great your entrance is, then the bell rings and you better know how to wrestle or you won't last long.

Everybody that's worth a shit will eventually be looked at. When your time comes, you better be ready. Nobody but you to blame if you're not sharp.

Facials, intensity, body language, timing, psychology, footwork, ring awareness and placement added to basics and promos can't go wrong.

What a body, what a gimmick, what an entrance, what gear. Unfortunately, then the bell rings. Don't let it be you.

If you're not confident in the ring on a certain move or bump, then don't do it. Hesitation means trouble for you or your opponent. Do something different.

One of the hardest things in the business is to throw good looking, working punches. Jabs, power punch, uppercut, gut punch. Most too lazy to practice.

If your hand is not in "Chop shape" after 3 chops, your hand is worse than the guys chest you are chopping.

Some guys you don't like until you work with them. Then there are guys you like until you work with them. The nature of the beast.

It takes awhile to learn to relax in the ring. Guys puke, hyper ventilate, and get so nervous over thinking when they are starting out. Relax kid, relax.

Some emotion and intensity looking like you're going to kick somebody's ass is a sure way to get fans to buy in to your match. 99 moves you don't sell doesn't.

You don't have to say a word that you're eating right and training. The mirror doesn't lie.

If you're overweight, don't be. If you're underweight, don't be. Get real boots and gear. Learn all different styles. Be different, Call it in the ring.

The styles may change, the stars may change, but it's still the greatest sport in the world to me. I will always be a kid around it.

If you ever really get this shit, It's beautiful. You are the conductor leading the orchestra to its peak before reaching the finale.

It takes no talent to hit or kick somebody hard. Learn your craft. Once you do, it's like riding a bike.

Nothing like being a rookie in the locker room and you're dressing with your heroes. Happy, scared, nervous, you name it. But what memories.

Lock yourself in the bathroom for an hour and cut promos. Use that mirror. Face and heel. Different characters.

I don't care what move, spot, or false finish it is, if you keep repeating the same stuff fans have already seen, it's not interesting. Be different.

Refs, if guys ignore your count to the floor, go out there and restart the count or threaten DQ. Work with them so they are not out there too long.

If you're in management, stop being a wrestler unless it's to elevate somebody and put them over to help the company. Forget your ego and be a mentor.

The bottom line is everything in any business. Same in wrestling. The boss pushes who he thinks will make the company a profit. He's the boss.

If fans yelled boring in Ronnie Garvin's match, he would say "I'll show them boring." Then he would sell a hold till it was "Come on Ronnie!"

The wrestlers are supposed to be the maestros in the ring leading the fans to peaks and valleys. They run the show, not the fans.

In ICW, Randy Savage glared at me and said" You know why I'm the champ? Because you're the best I said. "No, because my dad owns the territory. He said.

I remember Chris Benoit wanting me to teach him to work my style because he was killing himself and I barely broke a sweat. He was beat up.

Tall wrestlers stand next to short guys to make them look taller. Well built wrestlers stand next to skinny guys to make you look better.

If pro wrestling is your passion, learn it right. Respect all forms and try to learn psychology of each style. Protect each other.

Why did you do that in your match? It doesn't make any sense. But you don't get it, it's a really cool move and they say this is awesome.

Most Indy shows are like pick up basketball games in the park. Me, me oriented because you have limited time. Bad basics and fundamentals wanting to get all your shit in because it might be awhile until the next one. I get it, you love wrestling. Just be safe as you will get hurt because it's wrestling.

If everybody is doing clotheslines, super kicks. And dives, great. Just do something else they haven't seen and have them really sell it.

Learn your craft. If you really understand it. You will know how to work face and heel both even though one is your preference.

If your finish is a certain move and somebody uses it as a non finisher, great! Makes them look weak while fans think of you as yours working.

Wrestling is not brain surgery, we don't need to reinvent the wheel. Just give me two guys with a reason to beat the hell out of each other.

There are more marks in the dressing rooms than in the bleachers. If you want to do dangerous shit, do MMA. This is an art. An illusion.

As a pro you have to be able to work a giant as well as a short guy, a huge guy or a skinny one, a hard 24 ft ring or 14 ft one.

Buddy Rose was the top heel in Portland for 7 years. When he turned face he could have been mayor. Same with Roddy Piper. More hate=more love.

When you work with a green guy remember how nervous he probably is. Make it as simple as possible so he gains some confidence. Help him out.

Get you some nice gear and real pro wrestling boots. Look the part. Don't look like you belong in the audience. Look like somebody.

Watch the matches before yours. Don't repeat what's already been done. This is simple when you know how to call it in the ring.

If your promos lack, it's on you to get better. Look into that mirror and own it! Be as creative as you can in different characters. You can do it.

If you can talk shit and look great, that's fantastic! Now just make sure you can back it up with your wrestling ability. Be the total package.

Some things in wrestling you're real good at. So bust your ass working on the things right now you're bad at and make them your specialties.

Don't take liberties in the ring with new guys. You were a greenhorn once yourself. Show all you can be a leader.

Learn to adjust your dial in the ring. Whether you're light, ok, snug, or stiff is determined by your foe. Be able to change.

The object is to get in, get out, don't get hurt. Either you or your opponent. Sell each other, protect each other, fight another day.

When it's your time to be seen, be ready. Don't let it be "I wished I had dieted, trained, went to class, practiced my promos, etc."

The more you work with rookies the better you will get. You're forced to do basics and sell more.

Learn to cut promos on the fly. As face or heel in as many characters you can think of. Be a master at this and you're so much ahead of the curve.

Feel the crowd, the emotion, the atmosphere, learn to call a match in the ring. Watch the others and do something they haven't seen yet.

Guys that get it can handle any situation. Ring breaks, cut time, add time, get injured? No big deal. You don't get it? You're lost.

Learning to call a match in the ring on the fly is an art. Ring breaks, time is cut or extended, opponent gets hurt, no big deal. You got it.

If you really understand the business you can work face or heel because you understand the psychology of both in a pro wrestling match.

Don't be afraid to say no. If there is something in the ring you do not do well, don't do it. The heel should know another way to get same result.

If a guys is to duck your punch, clothesline, elbow, or whatever, throw it straight and to potato him. It's his job to duck. If not, too bad.

Dropkicks the shits? Simple. Do 400 of them and you will be the dropkick king. Turn a weakness into a strength with work, work, and more work.

Learn every aspect, and style you can. You may master a certain area of expertise but the opening is elsewhere. Be as well rounded as you can.

In any sport you improve your game and earn your spot in practice. You play the game the way you practice. Without practice, there is no game.

In wrestling they have to either love you or hate you. No middle ground. Then you're the popcorn match. Which is great if you have concessions.

Seriously look in the mirror, just eating correctly and working out you can transform your body in only 16 weeks. If you look bad, it's on you.

The art of the promo; you need your bullet points. Get your point across in character. Be you in your facials, body language, mannerisms, just be you.

Always tuck your boot laces in. If wearing a t shirt at practice, always tuck it in. Practice in your wrestling boots, not other shoes.

Please don't ever let anyone blade you. Seen too many bad things happen too many times.

It takes no skill to hit or kick somebody hard. But to make it look like it killed them and you didn't touch them. That is the art.

Go to the matches like you go to a game. Enjoy it. Don't over analyze it. Cheer, boo, laugh, scream, eat some junk, be a kid again. Have fun!

Stop your bitchin. You got your health, food, a job, a vehicle, roof over your head, and your gimmick phone. You got it better than most. Count your blessings, and pump the arms too.

You will be in the best wrestling shape and your fundamentals at their finest when you're going to wrestling class. You got to have someone pushing you to be the best you can be. You can't mentally do it on your own. Coaches make you the best you can be. Keep working.

On wearing lifts; If you're 5'7 two inch lifts still make you only 5'9. But by wearing those lifts you eliminate your strengths of quickness, coordination, and explosiveness. Play to your strengths. If you're great, it will shine through. Do your thing. Be your best.

The business didn't really change. People are the same. Today's wrestlers unfortunately don't have the opportunity to work 6-7 days a week in territory system and be led by real vets to learn to call it in the ring. To learn different regional styles and to be different characters.

Fans go to all sporting events, wrestling included, to see their favorites win and hope his opponent gets his ass kicked. Cheer, boo, don't matter, just let it be a full house and make the money.

First learn how to wrestle, then learn how to work, then learn every style u can, learn every trick and shortcut in the book. Learn both sides. Learn why and why not. Protect your opponent and live to see another day. Be a wrestler.

I've taught pro wrestling for over 20 years. The body, the gear, the gimmick, the promo, the moves, are the easy part. The psychology is the hard part. The placement of all this is very complicated. Very few learn it. Those that do are the best.

If you're trying to be a pro wrestler, but you don't eat right, workout, get as much ring time as you can, practice promos, punches, chain daily, get good gear including real wrestling boots, be addicted to wrestling on Youtube, then you're wasting your time. All or nothing.

You want to get good at any job, sport, playing in band, or cooking burgers? The key is consistency and always train or practice with those that are much better than you. You don't get good being one eyed king in the valley of the blind.

Once you give up on your dream there's really no hope. You settle, you wonder what if, you wished you would have given 100% Depression sets in, you drink, you smoke, you get fat. Because you never really know what if.

Try and help those with less experience than you. Even if you're going for same goal. If they make it they will always remember you and help you. If you're cutthroat to them, karma will get your ass eventually. Assholes will get it in the end.

If your music and entrance is the highlight of your match you are in trouble. Your wrestling should overshadow your entrance, not vice versa.

Meeting a new wrestler and having a real good match site unseen is such a great feeling.

I never watched a game to critique it, but to enjoy it. Same with watching TV or a movie, to forget real world problems. If you have time to overthink wrestling, you must lead a nothing happening life. I got shit to do and don't think about someone's push or lack of.

You are over when you draw. Noise and reaction means nothing. Plants, shortcuts, etc, mean nothing if you're in an empty building. You sell out, you're over. Bottom line. Put me on a quiet sellout any day, and you control the audience, not vice versa.

Guys get over because the lead announcer puts them over. If they are busy pushing diva show, Tuff Enuf, ppv, another WWE show, you won't get over. It's up to VKM to get the announcers to make it you, you, and more you to get over.

Don't repeat a spot if you mess it up. If you botch the finish, please don't immediately do it again.

Stay off the house mic unless you are told. Never touch the ref unless you are told. On a 3 count make sure both your shoulders are clearly down for allotted time. Never touch the manager or valet unless you are told. Don't go over your time limit. If need be, go shorter.

If you are using a manager or valet, try and let them go out there only once. The more they see them, the less they mean. If they are seen too much, they lose their heat. Keep each one special. Don't ever touch a manager or valet unless you are told to.

In any match, never touch a ref unless you are told to by the boss. The boss knows what he's doing down the line. You don't. If there is only one ref in the show, you need him 100% for all the matches. So always respect him, unless you're told not to.

When you're putting somebody over, don't kick out at 3. Make sure your shoulders are down for full 3 count. Don't put foot in ropes right at 3. Do it right, unless boss tells you to for an angle.

You don't do stuff in the ring just to do it. Hopefully you will learn what to do, when to do it, and why you do it. This isn't brain surgery but it's an art you have to put your time in before the light bulb goes off and you start to get it.

It's all the little things, paying attention to details that make a great worker. The moves are the easiest thing to learn. Placing them in each situation and knowing what to do is the art. Get in get out don't get hurt is a must in this business.

You can't ever go wrong with basics. Selling each other as a "contest." Throw in some emotion, intensity, body language, and you got yourself the makings of a good one.

Your opponent is giving you his body, it's your job to protect it. I would rather hurt myself than my opponent. If you're a guy hurting greenhorns, you're a real fucking asshole. You're not really a badass. You ain't Angle, Brock, Hodge, etc. It's a work asshole.

Dear young wrestlers, always try to remember how the world looked through your eyes as a child. Treat your young fans with this memory in mind. – Cody Deaner

You want to stand out? Be different? Do nothing outlandish. Every match has a dive, now it's nothing special. Instead show me some facials, body language, and intensity. Make them believe yours is a contest and you're gonna whoop his ass! Very simple.

What is great worker? Be able to work heel or face, call it in the ring and have good match from opener to main with who you work with in slot you're in. Be able to push strengths and hide weaknesses of foes. Look, talk, character, gear, needs to be great.

Stop slapping your leg on each kick, drop kick, etc. It's embarrassing. Marks making fun of it.

Once you go to practice with guys, make trips, and have matches with them, there is a special bond that will never be broken. Normal people can't and won't ever understand this. They are not one of us.

It's always nice to hear how hated you were as a heel years ago. You were doing your job correctly. Nothing like boos, jeers, spit and stuff thrown at you to let you know you're the man they love to hate. Thank you very much.

You can't play any sport at a high level without practice. You are fooling yourself if you think you can Practice is where you work on your weakness' to make them your strengths. Games and performances are won in practice.

Don't be doing wild and crazy shit unless you are making money. Chances of being hurt are easier doing high risk and if you get hurt, who pays your bills while you're out? Forget ego, think rationale. Think professional wrestler.

A face that really sells correctly makes the match so, so, easy. Too many want to stay strong. Everybody loves the underdog. Heels that want to do cool moves and want cheers need to be a baby face. It's not that complicated.

I never liked working towards the hard camera because it looks like you're doing just that. I liked the hand helds to have to find me and give fans unusual shots and angles.

When a face wants to get all his shit in, just let him. Have him cover you each time and just kick out on one. Then when it's time for heat, just stop him. You took all his shit then stopped him. He will eventually figure it out. I hope.

Look in the mirror, it doesn't lie. Do you look like something special? If not, do something about it. Your chances are better to make it looking great. You wanna see a fat or skinny stripper or one with a great body? Hhhmmmm...

A lot of people start in wrestling school, soon find out it's a whole lot more difficult than they could ever imagine. If it was easy anybody could do it.

There are a lot of talented performers out there in today's wrestling world. Men and women. Unfortunately there are few spots open and none will be unless others get hurt or released. It's not 1983 where 800 wrestlers worked full time in USA and Canada

You want to work strong style? Then get into MMA or be a boxer. It takes talent to do it the proper way. Takes zero ability to hit or kick somebody hard.

Old school wrestling heels were heels. You didn't sign autographs, chat with fans, or sell any pics, etc, you were the bad guy. You acted like it. Couldn't take it? Be a good guy! Good vs evil drew. Very basic, very simple, it worked.

Some people make an excuse for everything. But the ones that succeed overcome every barrier placed in front of them.

Nothing a coach likes to see more than his students giving their all to pursue their dreams. You're like a proud father watching his kids succeed. Makes you feel really good.

How much practice time does it take to play in NBA, NFL, MLB? Takes your whole day it seems like. You want to be a

WWE superstar? Training consistently with that kind of effort is your best chance to be there.

If you're being overlooked, eat better, train more, get in ring as much as possible, practice promos, and punches as much you can. Get there early, leave late, help others. Soon you won't be overlooked.

Never apologize for loving pro wrestling. You gotta be nuts not to love it. Where else will you see people fighting in their undies?

You bust your ass in practice to iron out all the kinks. Practice is where you put in the work so when it's game time you are physically and mentally ready.

You're over when you got a sellout. Pops are for marks. Reaction is usually shortcuts. Work to get your match over and not to pop the dressing room.

Wrestlers never retire. They just don't get booked anymore.

You get in the biz and you find out the bad guys are usually really the good guys, and the ones with the belts are often carried by the jobber.

As you get older you remember all the stupid shit you did earlier in life and try to help others not to make same mistakes, but they will anyway.

WWE will give you a character, finisher, song, special big move. Just look great and master the basics and practice those promos.

Greenhorns, don't worry about cool moves, your entrance music, your big finisher, your character, first learn to wrestle, wrestle, wrestle.

When I got in the wrestling business, the only school I heard of was Verne Gagnes. Now there are many schools to go to and they won't stretch you.

A pin attempt should mean something. The more you have, the less they mean. Just like punches, big moves, and bumps.

Do some serious soul searching. Has your physique changed for the better since you've been training? Have all aspects of your game increased? Go 100%

Some of the best times of your life is riding home after your match with vets telling stories and going over your match. This is where you learn.

Wrestling fans used to go to the matches to see the faces whip the heels ass. Now they come in to rate matches, see who is buried and who is pushed.

You're an athletic actor just playing a role. Have the time of your life with it. It's all a rib. Be as over the top as you can. Have fun.

Whatever needs to be done to put your opponent over playing to what he does well and concealing what he can't do.

Everybody that's worth a shit will eventually be looked at. When your time comes, you better be ready! Nobody but you to blame if you're not sharp.

I get upset with those who are lazy and miss class with excuse after excuse. I expect you to love this as I do and give 100% in each aspect of it.

As a heel it's up to you to be the QB in the ring. Each guy has different strengths and weaknesses and it's up to you to make him the best he can be.

All wrestling companies go through boom times and hard times. Just like any business. If Wrestlemania 1 was a flop, WWE would be hurting too.

Faces got the pretty girls, food, and presents from the fans. Made gimmick money and got cheers. Heels got spit on, tires slit, etc, but it was fun.

UFC does pro wrestling better than pro wrestling. Emotion, characters are themselves, promos from within. Just two guys that want to fight.

Today's wrestlers should know the history of our business. Performers worldwide, angles, territories, what is old is new again.

To get better you have to be continuously pushed harder. To get out of your comfort zone. You want to get better? Train with those better than you.

Doing too much before the main halts your push as you show you're not a team player. Do as boss asks to help the company. Cool moves anybody can do. What's your role? Get on base? Set that pick? Bust up that wedge? Hit the cutoff man? Block out? Hit behind the runner? Have a solid match

Wearing jewelry wrestling is a no no. No ear rings or necklaces once the bell rings. I saw Don Fargo rip a guy's ear almost off who did.

In wrestling you can't control politics. Who's related to who or how tall you are. But you can give 100% to your craft to be the best you can be.

Fans don't realize you do only what the boss says in character, promos, and in ring work. You do as told or get a real job. Reality of wrestling.

Title switches used to be a big deal. Way too many belts today. A champ means the number one wrestler. Who hasn't been a champ?

Be smart, if everybody is doing spots and coming off the top, do the opposite. It's a buffet. Give them some steak instead of chicken again.

As a fan you will see a match one way, as a wrestler you might have a different take on it. And as a promoter you will see it in a completely different form.

It takes awhile to learn to relax in the ring. Guys puke, hyper ventilate, and get so nervous over thinking when they are starting out.

Always appreciate and thank your trainers, as they tell you about the problems you're going to have and give you the solutions before you even have them!

Would you drive 200 miles one way to pick up s $50 bill then drive back where you came from? Hell no! Who in their right mind would do it? But for the love of wrestling you will drive that far just for the love of doing your thing in the ring. Money is great but passion is better!

When somebody puts you over the right way, make sure you thank them. And when roles are reversed, return the favor.

Years ago WWF would have Les Thornton have a long boring slow paced match before Hogan's so when fans heard HH music they went wild.

Feel the crowd, the emotion, the atmosphere, learn to call a match in the ring, watch the others and do something they haven't seen yet.

Learn to work different styles. Sometimes in boxing ring, 14 ft ring, or 24 ft ring. Some opponents gifted, some hardly smart. Learn to survive.

The ref explained the rules to the wrestlers before each match in the ring, that way the fans knew the rules and when the heel broke them.

OVW has sent 64 wrestlers, refs, writers, office people, to WWE, ROH, and IMPACT Wrestling, that came through the OVW doors chasing a dream on their dime.

When you tell people your goal is to be a WWE wrestler, they immediately knock you because you got enough balls to chase your dream and they don't. Show them all.

Moves don't make the wrestler, it's his ability to invoke emotion from the fans to want to see him win or lose.

One bad apple in the barrel can poison them all. Same in wrestling class. One shit attitude that thinks he knows it all hurts the others.

Girls you get better in the ring by training with guys. You hang with men you can excel with the girls. Always practice with guys better than you.

Wrestling is 50% look and promo. 20% work and 30% who you know or are related to. I didn't invent this, somebody else did.

Whipping someone into a turnbuckle always go past the half way mark of the ring.

When chopping, stay above the nipple, below neck. If you're taking the chop, relax, don't flex. More fat means more noise if done correctly.

When somebody is throwing you into the ropes, please stop feeding him your hand. It's embarrassing. Make him grab it.

A high spot should look like your reaction to your opponents move. Not like choreographed synchronized swimming. Looks phony.

Don't make things complicated. If you're winning, don't worry about getting your shit in. You're winning. If you're losing, take more so win means more.

When you get really good you can actually get fans to believe your match is real and the others aren't.

If you're in a wrestling school, have your coach teach you how to have a 30 min broadway babyface match.

At your school, have your coach teach you to have a one hour match. You will find out it's a lot easier than it sounds. Just class pieced together.

You used to have a two hour show with 4 matches. No music, no promos, guys knew how to work safely, be different, and pull time.

Have your coach teach you to have a one hour tag match with two heat segments. First heat with more holds so you save final comeback with strikes.

Try and learn at least one thing to do or not to do each match or practice. Most of your improvement comes in practice.

Every time you work in a ring, check the boards, turnbuckles, pads, ropes, fix any would be surprises where you could get hurt or hinder your match.

If you're on first, stay in the ring, limit your strikes, concentrate on basics. Yours sets the pace for the show. Doing too much hurts the show.

If a guy is a great wrestler, don't be jealous of him but use him as example of what you could be if you applied yourself 100%.

If the lead announcer is putting you over big time every second of the match you will get over. If he's talking divas, network, PPV, you won't.

As a wrestling fan you should hope ROH and Impact can stay profitable to give you more choices to watch and give wrestlers more jobs. Competition.

I seen so many wrestlers over analyzing everything. From their push, their gimmick, their match, their promos, they self destruct. Have fun.

All trainees today should watch old World of Sport TV show from England. You will see and hopefully learn from these greats. What's old is new.

Wrestling to me has always been about the trips to different lands, the characters you meet, the memories you create, the shenanigans, so unbelievable.

Sending a highlight tape to a promoter is ok if the promoter is a mark. I want to see a match to see if you get it. Moves are irrelevant. Do you get it.

Heels use rough, rugged strikes and double team moves. Faces do more wrestling double team moves. Save your strikes till the end in your comeback.

If practicing kicks to stomach, make sure your opponent has his shirt tucked in because I've seen too many knee surgeries where foot gets caught in shirt.

Don't use baby oil in the ring period. You're asking for trouble. Either you or opponent can slip and get hurt bad. Be safe at all times.

It's up to you to practice promos. You want this or not? It's part of job description today.

Always tuck the laces of your boots in. Saw a guy get blinded from boot lace hitting him in the eye on an enziguiri.

Most of the stars in wrestling that are really good are average size, with average athletic ability, but they have the heart and drive of a lion.

Train like you are trying to make the team, not like you already made it. Once you think you know it all, the start of the end is near.

Just do as you are asked to do by the boss. It's his money, his decision, his business. Any attitude can be adios amigo. Don't like it, start your own.

When you travel 500 miles, lose $100 but get to have a match in front of 36 fans and you are pumped for 24 hours, I think I know what your passion is.

A lot of people say they want it, but how many are really willing to put in the work to make it? Thousands have the same dream. Can you do it?

You can practice promos anywhere. Face or heel. Change characters, facials, emotion, body language, vary volume, and pace.

First match, don't go outside, limit your strikes, don't put heat on the ref this early, don't use gimmick, no managers please, jus wrestle.

What's bad about wrestling is; all walk the same, talk the same, wrestle the same, look the same, be different. Learn different psychologies.

Please learn at least 5 different covers to pin somebody. Don't give your left hand to somebody when you're going to take a turnbuckle or thrown into ropes. Make them grab it. Please learn to sell away and not face the guy.

Once you go to a good wrestling school to learn, you're going to find out it's nothing the way you thought it was and it's a whole lot harder.

Was told I couldn't train every body part every day, so I did for nine years. Was told I couldn't have a pro boxing fight at 41, so I did. I was told I couldn't be a wrestler, so I did. I was told I couldn't get in a physique contest, so I got in 12 in 18 months. Won two, clean.

Just starting out? Invest in real wrestling boots, not tennis shoes. Real leather wrestling boots, expensive but worth it.

I blow you up so when it's time to think and execute your finish you will be able to think and perform with no problem. You tired? You can't perform.

There is no "one way" to teach pro wrestling. Just like any sport, learn as many methods, styles, philosophies, as you can to up your game.

The object in wrestling is to draw money without anybody getting hurt. Not to do stupid dangerous shit in front of 35 fans for free.

Your spot is determined by the boss. Do as he asks right and he will have confidence to move you up on the card because he can trust you.

Brock Lesnar drove the ring truck at OVW, while John Cena, Randy Orton, set up the ring. Learn your business. Inside and out.

If your goal is to be a wrestler and your other half doesn't support you 100%, better get a new significant other. You have one goal and you need 100% support.

You can't make class because you have personal and financial issues but you can make a show 3-4, hours away. Facebook stooges you off.

Buddy rose in Portland in a two out of 3 fall match would give up to a simple head lock or arm bar from too much pain.

The best way to get in shape for pro wrestling is wrestle. Bike, stepper, squats, are good, but to get in shape wrestle.

Wrestling should be like the circus, different entertaining acts. Every match should not be the same. Each should be different. Different style, different look.

When you are getting heat on your opponent your body language should be in attack mode. Facials, and body language. Not looking like a waltz in the park.

We wrestled in Hannover, Germany 70 days in a row in 1992. Fans had season tickets. Would save all year to buy them. Couldn't do the same old stuff, had to be good then.

In pro wrestling, the diet, class, and physical part is the easy part. The mental toughness is the one that sets you apart from the field.

Talent in wrestling is being able to work face or heel safely with anybody for the slot you are in, pulling whatever time is needed.

When I'm screaming at you I want you to "get it." If I stop yelling at you, that means I gave up on you. How was my match? Fantastic.

You make your mistakes in practice so you won't make them in the game. Match time is not time to try something new. Your game is practice just pieced together. Eventually you see it. But for a long time you won't get it. Most quit long before they get it. The moves are the easy part.

If you don't like the way pro wrestling is being run, please start your own promotion with your own money. You will see how hard it is to draw now.

The most important part about practice is being there.

Some like brawls, high spots, big ass flippy doos, great competitive chain wrestling, many false finishes, no matter what, we all like rasslin. Lucha, Hardcore, gimmick matches. All different flavors of ice cream as Dr. Tom would say.

The problem with guys going to class is they can call it in the ring, ad lib with no problem and salvage pretty much anything in the ring. The problem is when they work with guys that don't go to class they are held back because the guy that doesn't practice is way behind.

If your goal is to be a pro wrestler and your girl doesn't support you 100%, just get another girl. You got one dream.

Pressed for time? Get up earlier. Costs no more to eat healthy. Cut promos while driving or in the bathroom. A set of 50 push-ups takes 1 minute.

I didn't make the rules but you got a better chance to make it if you are jacked, tan, good gear, go to different seminars keep getting better. It's on you.

You have to be half crazy to be a wrestling fan, and completely crazy to be a wrestler. But what's wrong with crazy?

In a match, let's say both are fighting on the floor. You have a 20 count, one rolls in, count stops for him but it should continue for other. Should be a count out on the 2nd guy who was still selling. WWE has made all rules shit.

How are you supposed to be the best without practicing? You just don't show up for the games. Skills deteriorate and mediocrity is your destination.

We killed our own product. Doing too much in the ring, taking all believability out of it. Sadly it's now a rib and a stunt show.

The NWA title match was always best 2 out of 3 falls so champ and challengers finish hold actually worked for a pin or submission in a match.

Trying to be a pro wrestler with no real consistent training is like saying "I'm going play in NBA but I don't want to practice."

Safety is the most important aspect of pro wrestling. Your opponent should never be in danger of getting hurt when in the ring with you.

In pro wrestling you will be asked to do many things and perform many roles. Do all to the best of your ability. Face or heel. Do it right with no ego.

You get over with the bosses by doing your role correct. If they want you over strong, do it. If your to be squashed, do it. Forget your ego.

Don't be a mark and pout when the office tells you to put somebody over. They know the long range plan. Do it to the best of your ability.

As a performer, first you learn to lose humbly. Then you learn to win. Double humbly.

A great ref can save a shitty match and a shitty ref can kill a great match. Ref is a very important part of the match.

I've worked in 14 foot rings in England and 24 foot boxing rings in South Africa and every size in between. Each one is different to work in.

A lot of people say it's there dream to make it in pro wrestling. It's not a dream, it's a lot of hard work and sacrifice.

Don't kid yourself, you are going to be sore and get hurt being a wrestler.

Pops, noise, reaction, mean nothing in a match. When you are really interested, you are mesmerized by the contest in the ring. Completely engaged.

Learn as many styles as you can. Go to as many seminars as you can. Look at old matches on Youtube. Especially World of Sport.

Don't worry about how many moves you get in. Work on how, when, and why you do them. Tell a story a kid can understand and you will be doing fine.

First impression is everything. If you are skinny or fat, get your ass in gear. Looking like an athlete is a must to get noticed in most cases.

Look like a pro, get some nice trunks, robes, real wrestling boots, nice hair, tan, shaved.

Pretty much all your family, friends, and acquaintances will knock you and think you're crazy for pursuing your real dream, Be prepared for it.

If you're on second, watch the first one. Whatever they do, don't do it. No need to repeat something already seen.

Wrestling in Durbin South Africa having a riot 3 Saturday's in a row was quite an accomplishment to being a heel.

Riots two weeks in a row at TV in Puerto Rico was good to keeping you sharp and being ready for anything. Knives, bottles, etc.

Richlands, VA and Montgomery, Alabama fans pulled guns out on me. You know you did your job well as a heel. What a rush controlling the match. When the heels would be fighting to get back to the dressing room after a hot heel finish. Fans trying to literally kill them. Today's fans will never get to experience and feel the atmosphere of pro wrestling. Where the girls would be crying when the face is selling.

8 hours at a real job is horrible. But working 36 straight hours travelling, wrestling trip, is like a vacation. Your passion is not a job.

Have a 30 min face Broadway. A 1 hour match. A one hour babyface tag. One hour tag, all called in the ring. You do these, you pretty much got it.

A wrestling show should be like the circus. Giant, midget, sword swallower, fat man, skinny man, bearded lady, juggler, three legged man, all unique.

Basketball fans, you see that dunk? That 3, what a crossover and step back, nice euro! Uh we lost by 30. But there were cool moves. Wrestling?

The adventures you have as a pro wrestlers will keep a shit eating grin on your face forever. Feel bad? Just think back, chuckle, and smile.

Working in Nashville for Gulas, The Rocks Dad Rocky Johnson came to my room to see if I wanted to go eat because The Rock was hungry. I didn't know who he was talking about. Took awhile for me to realize he was talking about himself. So The Rock stole his dad's gimmick. Nothing is original.

Learn every aspect of wrestling you can. You never know when your time will come and in what capacity to get your foot in the door. Be ready baby!

A real fat guy can lose 50 lbs, still look fat, but oh "He looks great" A bodybuilder gains or loses some weight and its "Are you sick?"

Years ago it was no big deal to go 30 or more in a tag or single with somebody you never seen before. All knew basics and heels just called it.

Learn to ref. Might be a way to the big time. Plus you will get more ring time. See and feel the action up close and understand it even more.

Reality: the average career of a WWE superstar is like that of NFL running back. Nothing lasts forever. So do your best and enjoy your dream.

If you are considered short in the wrestling business, even with those stupid lifts on your boots, you're still short. But you take away your asset of quickness and coordination by hindering yourself. Play to your strengths.

How many different kind of strikes do you know without repeating? How many different holds for the stomach do you know? Neck? Back? Counters? How many holds for the leg do you know how to apply? Counters? How many different holds and counter holds for the arm do you know?

You get more conditioning, fundamentals, basics, reps, in one class than you do in a month of matches. Make mistakes in class, not in the event.

When you make it, always remember that little boy in you that idolized the wrestlers. Remember what it was to be a fan. Give them your time. Give back.

I've been in the ring and the top rope breaks, boards break in ring, Whole ring collapses, ring fails to arrive. Wrestle on the floor. Pro handles it all.

If it's your job to put someone over, do it the right way. Don't worry about your offense. It's your job to make your opponent look great.

The Rock's people's elbow shows how you can get anything over. It's a rib. But he gets that. Get in, get out, don't get hurt, go home.

It's up to you to protect your finish hold. Never let anyone escape unless the money man says so.

When your boss tells you to do something, just do it. You don't know the long range plan. If I can't trust you to lose correctly, how can I trust you as a top guy? Do as asked to the best of your ability. Be a team player. Do that and your time will probably come because they trust you.

Was on my way to Louisville gardens to wrestle 1986. There a block away was Muhammad Ali giving out free bibles. I took my shirt off and cut a promo on him. He didn't miss a beat, cut one on me, gave me a personalized autographed bible and drew wrestling ring too.

I don't have to work out I WANT to work out!

The wrestlers that have a passion for this business will still be involved with it 20 years from now, with money not mattering.

Most everything in wrestling is a test. Does he listen? Does he really understand? Can he ad lib? Does he do the job right with no qualms? Can he be trusted on live TV? Does he get the product over more than worrying about himself? Is he a positive force in the locker room?

Dives, too many moves, excessive strikes, will come and go. But the art of pro wrestling if done correctly, will live forever. Facials, body language, emotion, and intensity get an audience going every time and always will.

What is a great worker? Someone who is able to work heel or face, call it in the ring, and have a good match from opener to main. Be able to push strengths and hide weaknesses of foes. Look, talk, character, gear, needs to be great.

Doing a million moves in a match means nothing. You obviously can't beat him. Intensity, emotion, selling, fighting back, a contest.

HUSTLER RIP ROGERS

The final sections of this book is for people that have decided to start their own promotion, will work as a booker, or pro wrestling trainer.

Promoters / booking

There's no qualifications to be a wrestling promoter. If you got money it's yours to learn with, but it's a long hard expensive road to learn.

When you're a promoter you're the one taking the financial risk. Whatever you guarantee the workers, you should have that set aside. You pay them their guarantee no matter what. If it bombs, they get their money. But if it's sellout you owe them just their guarantee.

There are two kinds of promoters: one is a perfectionist, demanding, strict as hell. Wants you to do as told, and he pays you well. Other is friendly, funny, let's you do what you want, puts you over, and pays you little. Which do you want to work for?

A wrestling card should be structured to start with basics and solid finishes and build with each match getting a little more freedom. The Main Event should be treated as such, giving closure to the show. You want them standing at the end, not in the 3rd match.

The general rule of wrestling is; 1st match they haven't seen anything yet so really stress basic holds, stay in the ring, try not do too many strikes if any. Don't milk or use a gimmick. No big moves unless it's finish. Limit false finishes.

It's not the job of leadoff hitter to hit home runs, it's to get on base. It's not the job of underneath matches to try and outdo the main event. It's to have a solid basic match, different from what fans have already seen. Let the main do their job.

Always give the fans a solid first match, it sets the pace of the show. You can disguise a 2nd match as the fans have already seen good basic wrestling, but don't start the show off with a subpar match, will be harder to recover from for the rest of the matches.

When booking, don't have two similar matches in a row unless you have to, like a tag team tournament. No 2 high flyer matches in a row. Be special.

There is only one WWE. Other companies don't copy them, but develop your own brand. Make them want to copy you instead of being WWE lite. Create your own stars with many different styles.

Try and keep your wrestling shows to 2 hours max. Any more the butt gets numb, like a movie, crowd is exhausted. Make them sad it's over and can't wait to come back instead of punishing them and not wanting to come back because it's too long.

Promoters and bookers are supposed to be wise. Don't allow your workers to do dangerous stupid moves where they might get hurt. If you allow it, you are part of the problem. They will do anything to get a pop, but you need to protect them.

If there are dives in every match, now you're doing the same as everybody else. Set yourself apart. Be different. Anything old is new again to a new audience.

Emotion is what draws money in any sport. Floyd vs Connor, Yankees vs Red Sox, Pats vs Colts, IU vs Purdue, Cavs vs Golden state. Emotion.

Upsets and underdogs winning is what makes sports beautiful and a must see. When will wrestling start to get it? You should not know who's going to win,. but it should be "I hope he wins." Upsets gets fans talking and paying more attention. So simple. Treat it as a sport.

Always book a match you know will be shitty right before the main event. Main event will then look so much better.

Years ago, WWF would have Les Thornton have a long boring slow paced match before Hogan's so when fans heard HH music they went wild.

As a booker when you bump a ref he can: A. Stay down and sell. B. Get up after small sell. C. Another ref comes in to finish match. D. Another ref comes in but downed ref waves him off and continues match. E. Ref just shook it off and continued. F. New ref came in and finished the match. Ref bump in last match only.

If I'm in the office I'm not wrestling anymore. You're in the office because you're done, old, seen your act, Your job is to help others not hold back.

Rasslin 101.. The more belts you have the less they mean. The more belt switches you have the less they mean. Have face chase heel.

If I'm booking a handicap match, an intergender match, or a gauntlet match, two men vs one that are pros would beat the one. The man would destroy the woman, and would have so much heat he would draw next time against one who saved her. In a gauntlet match, guy will get destroyed after maybe one win. These are pros, they would then destroy him. You got to have some reality booking.

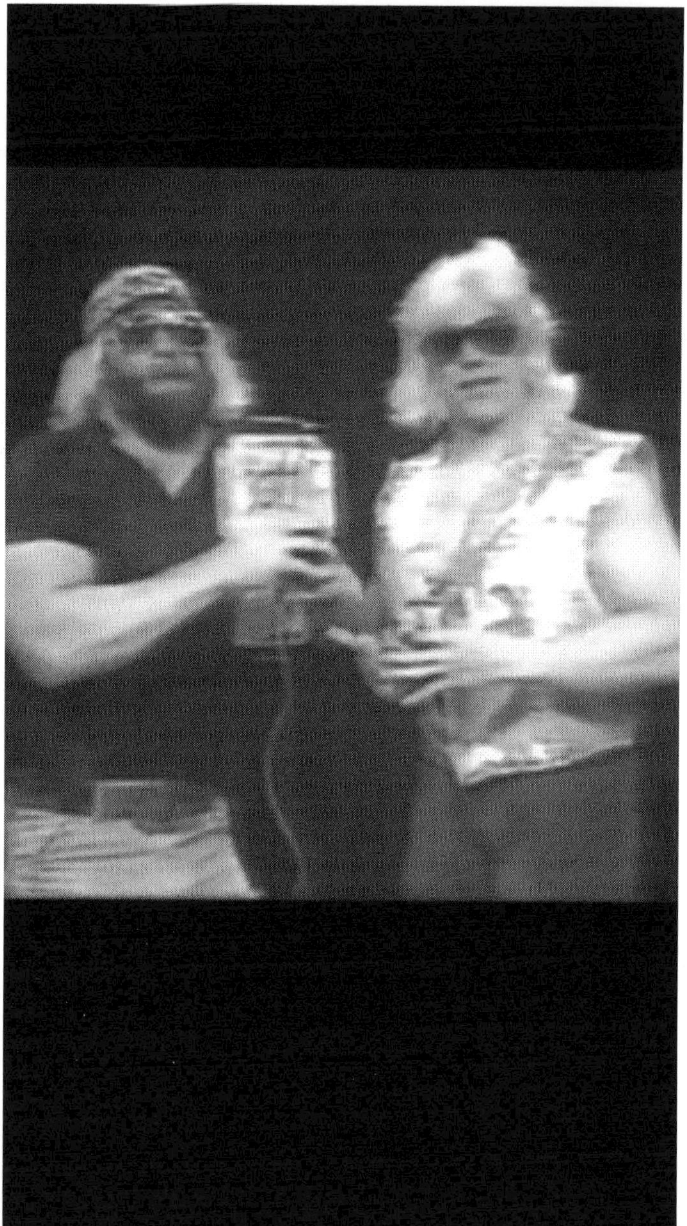

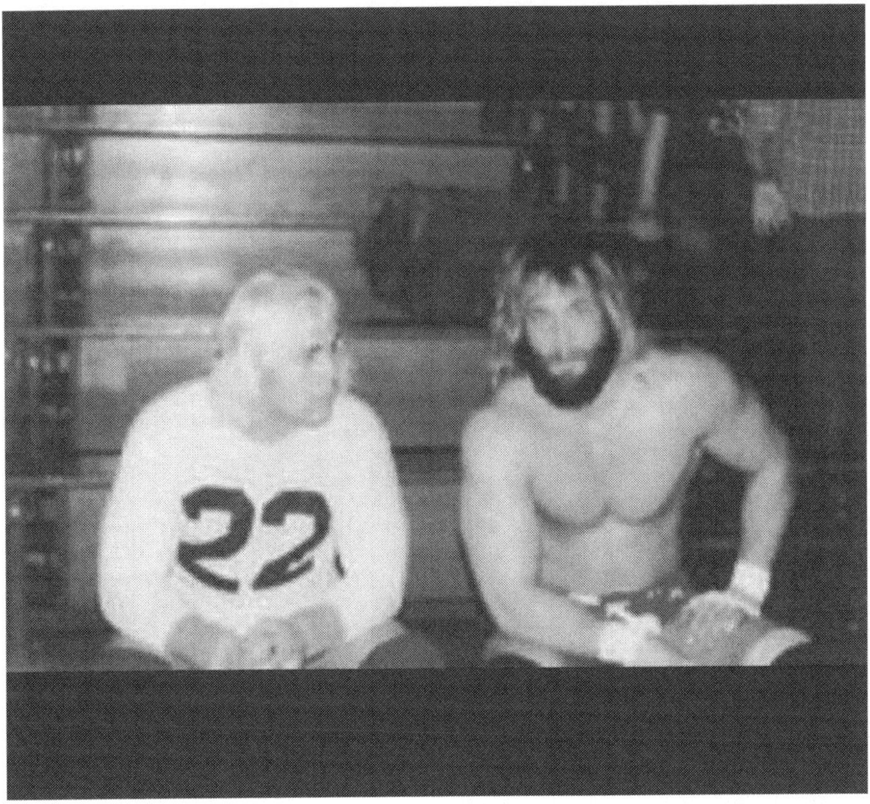

Trainers

I don't know about you, but I get the opportunity to help young wrestlers chase a dream today. Doesn't get any better than that.

As a coach, it's my duty to share every bit of knowledge I have in the business. All the tricks, in every aspect of the game to you. My job is to make you better than I ever was in all areas of our sport.

Players usually hate their coach when playing for him because he pushes you and calls you on your shit. Years later you finally get it.

Some guys are lucky and make a lot of money but share zero knowledge. It's your duty to help those coming up to keep the tricks passed down forever.

The goal of every wrestling coach should be to make his students better than he ever was at each and every aspect of pro wrestling. Everything in that old brain of yours should be shared to help mold the stars of tomorrow.

Remember all the wrestlers that helped you on your journey and try to help others the way they did you. Without vets there is no rasslin.

As a coach you should be humbled that these kids come to you to help them reach their dream. Always remember how hungry you were when you started.

You can train a lot of students, but only a very few are willing to do the work, make the sacrifices, and have the dedication to keep it up till they make it.

The more years you're around wrestling, the more you understand it. Same as in any job or sport. Coaches are old. Not 20. They've seen a lot failures and figured out the solutions. It's a labor of love when it's your passion.

Rip Rogers at the WCW Power Plant

I hope that by completing this book you have a new understanding and appreciation for pro wrestling and to those who have helped you along the way. To fully grasp what is contained on the pages previously, keep this book handy as you continue your training and working as a pro wrestler. Mark the pages however you need to so that you may quickly read through it again and refresh your mind on the most important points to you. Share what you have learned in this book with other fellow wrestlers. Discuss specific topics mentioned here and get an idea of other points of view. There is no absolute one correct way of wrestling. There are many different styles, and fans demand variety. It is my hope that this book helped you to understand a less talked about and even less used style and philosophy of wrestling and will allow you to have a greater career because of it.

A few last words

Simply reading what is written here is not enough. You must be able to implement this information in training and in matches. There are many great schools to learn pro wrestling, but the majority of them will focus primarily on executing moves, rather than the reasoning behind them.

OVW (Ohio Valley Wrestling) is still to this day, the best place to learn pro wrestling and provides the greatest opportunities for aspiring pro wrestlers. More people have been hired to WWE and other top promotions than any other pro wrestling school out there. OVW has been so successful that now its alumni students are opening wrestling schools of their own all over the world, and teaching the OVW way.

Andy Baker also a long time student of OVW and Rip Rogers and his RWA (Runcorn Wrestling Academy) in the UK has multiple schools now and has been running strong for many years teaching the OVW way. Visit rwawrestlinguk.com for more information.

As people continue to move to Louisville, KY from all over the world to train at OVW, there is surely to be more schools teaching the OVW way in the future.

Acknowledgments

If not for so many people, this book would not exist. But the most key people in the creation of this book I have to point out specifically.

First off I would like to thank Danny Davis. The founder and mastermind of OVW for so many years. Because of him and his creation, many have had the opportunity to make their dreams come to life and not only pursue their passion of becoming a pro wrestler, but to go on and become very successful. Those that have been successful have been able to provide for their families and inspire millions across the globe.

Andy Baker my wrestling classmate who gave me the inspiration to start my own wrestling school and promotion to begin teaching students what we both learned together in Rip's class.

Al Snow for continuing to build OVW and create opportunities for those interested in careers in pro wrestling.

And of course Rip Rogers for pushing me to be the best all those years in training and passing on the knowledge in such a way that you couldn't forget. Those that have trained with Rip will understand exactly what this means.

To learn more or begin your career as a wrestler, please visit the links below.

OVW (Ohio Valley Wrestling) – ovwrestling.com

RWA (Runcorn Wrestling Academy) – rwawrestlinguk.com

DPW (Dubai Pro Wrestling) – dubaiprowrestling.com

Made in the USA
Columbia, SC
02 December 2018